CRUSHING SATAN'S HEAD

THE VIRGIN MARY'S VICTORY OVER THE ANTICHRIST FORETOLD IN THE OLD TESTAMENT

FR JAMES MAWDSLEY

NEW OLD

Cover: Caravaggio (1571-1610), *Madonna dei Palafrenieri*

Published by New Old
© 2022 Fr James Mawdsley
ISBN 978-1-7395816-1-9

But Mary kept all these words, pondering them in her heart.

— Lk 2:19

FOR MY SISTER

Contents

THE VIRGIN MARY'S VICTORY

T he chief purpose of this work is to inspire invincible confidence in God. He will certainly accomplish the salvation which He first promised in Eden and has promised again and again ever since. Nothing that happens on earth or elsewhere, nothing, should dissuade us of that.

The method for encouraging this confidence is to ponder a dozen Old Testament (OT) stories which foretell the final victory of good over evil. All of these stories point to the Blessed Virgin Mary as God's chosen instrument for the triumph. And they call as well for our participation, regardless of how long we live before the end times.

Only God can lay down typology in the Scriptures. Catholic saints have found multiple cases, recorded over thousands of years, converging with perfect harmony on the Blessed Virgin Mary. Recognition of their first fulfilment two thousand years ago gives us unshakeable certainty that they will be finally fulfilled in her again at the end of time. That is to say, OT typology, consummated centuries later in the New Testament (NT), provides a sure demonstration that the endgame is already sealed — once we see that the first fulfillment is a pledge of the final one. God tells us what we need to know to secure salvation. As the labour pains of the end times grow more intense, so the Scriptures yield up more of their mysteries, knowledge for the safe delivery into the next life of those who have ears to hear in this one.

Typology, or the study of prefigurements, is a battlefield. Interpretations are hotly disputed because not everyone wishes to face what is at stake. A prefigurement is typically, but not exclusively, when a person, event or object in the OT has a hidden relation to Jesus Christ or to the mysteries and persons surrounding Him. Unlike prophecies and parables, the original author need not be aware that his text points to something greater. But by studying the literal sense of what is written, we may attain also a spiritual sense intended by the ultimate Author of Sacred Scripture, God. The various hidden meanings are revealed in the Light of Christ.

The NT makes clear that events from the OT have hidden meanings pertaining to salvation: Jesus teaches that Jonah spending three days in the belly of the whale prefigures His own three days in the tomb (Mt 12:40); St Peter explains the waters of the Flood prefigure baptism (1 Pet 3:20-21); St Paul writes Hagar and Sarah are an allegory for the Old Covenant and the New (Gal 4:24); St Jude identifies the fiery fate of Sodom as foreshadowing eternal damnation (Jude 7).

Following these writings from the Apostles, the Church Fathers show the Bible is inexhaustibly rich in layers of meaning, in spiritual senses which build on the literal. The Fathers rarely insist on their own interpretations, preferring to offer them only insofar as they might be useful. In humility they are ready for their personal understanding to be rejected. Even so, they give enough convincing examples that we may say the whole Bible is Christ, that not only the NT but even the OT includes His Death and Resurrection, His Sacraments, His Church, His saints and most importantly, His Mother.

Among the tremendous privileges of the Mother of God discernible in the OT is her final victory over the Antichrist. It is uniquely hers, yet we are all called to share in it. The beginning of that work is to believe.

I: CRUSHING SATAN'S HEAD

T he Mother of God is prefigured throughout the OT in persons, places and things. The Virgin Mary is glimpsed in Adam's helper, Eve. Her divine Motherhood is hinted at in the miraculous conceptions of the holy matriarchs Sarah, Rachel and Rebecca. Mary's humility is indicated in Ruth, and her royal authority in queen mothers from Bathsheba onwards. Mary's role in salvation is celebrated in the songs of Deborah, Miriam, Anna and Judith. Our Lady is typified by the virgin earth at Creation, by the sealed garden of the Canticle, by Mount Sion, by the burning bush, the ark of the covenant, the altar of incense, and that life-giving answer to the prophet's prayers seen from the top of Mount Carmel — the water-bearing cloud which broke the famine. St Bernard, who spiritually ascended Mount Carmel, identifies further treasures:

> Mary was the rootless rod of Aaron the Priest, which had not yet budded, yet brought forth buds, and blooms, and blossoms, and yielded almonds. She was the fleece of Gideon, which was put on the floor, and whereon only there was a dew when it was dry upon all the earth beside. She was the gate which Ezekiel saw, which looked toward the East and was shut, and the Lord said unto him: *'This gate shall be shut, it shall not be opened, and no man shall enter on by it'*.[1]

These fascinating types are hidden in the Scriptures by God so that we may seek them, and finding them be consoled, strengthened, and made alive in hope and wisdom. For the world is dark but God's Word is a lamp to our feet. Mary herself is the *"woman clothed with the sun"* (Apoc 12:1), that is, clothed with Christ, so that by her we may see even when night finally falls.

Each chapter of *Crushing satan's head* can be read on its own as a meditation on this theme. However, it is the connections between them, and the consistency of the whole, which should convince even the skeptic that the stories of the OT point to something far greater than is apparent at their first reading. For it was by God's Providence that the selected events first happened, and by His inspiration that they were

---

[1] St Bernard, *Sermon for Sunday in the Octave of the Assumption.*

recorded in the Scriptures, and by His protection and guidance that the texts have been preserved and distributed worldwide. His purpose thereby is to secure our salvation. Those who seek to understand, who ponder these words, will be confirmed in faith. Those who believe may stand firmly.

The first section below examines a promise God made to Adam and Eve in Eden. This is followed by seven foreshadowings of the promise's final fulfilment, namely Our Lady crushing satan's head, defeating the Antichrist. First, Jael, wife of Heber, pierced an antichrist's temple, his brains, with an apocalyptic tent peg. Second, the woman of Thebez smashed an antichrist's skull with a millstone. Next Jephthah's daughter immolated herself in a holocaust for the sake of her father's victory over the forces of evil. Then the wise woman of Abel saved her city by having an antichrist decapitated. Fifth, Judith famously cut off the enemy's head using his own weapon. Also Queen Esther's intercession saved her whole people and saw the wicked destroyed. Seventh, Susanna's purity, her preferring to die than to sin, brought a turnaround triumph over diabolical corruption of power.

The second section, entitled *Mary Pondered All these Words in Her Heart*, reflects on the likelihood that Our Lady found these foreshadowings first. As Mary's meditations upon Scripture would help her fulfil her calling perfectly, so we need recourse to Scripture too, in order to understand reality and within it our own calling.

The third section treats of four more women who *Announce the Annunciation*, relishing the richness of Sacred Scripture on the triumph of good over evil and the key role of the Woman in this triumph. Tamar can convince us not to judge by appearances but to appreciate there are unexpected mysteries known to the Woman, which in time she will share. Rahab underlines the absolute necessity of being within the Woman's household, being under Mary's mantle — those who follow her instructions will live while whoever departs from her household, *"his blood will be on his own head"* (Josh 2:19). In Ruth we encounter one of the most tender souls ever created, a picture of human nature perfected. If one wishes for a study of Our Lady's maternal care, of feminine efficacy, of sweetness of character, Ruth provides it. Bathsheba shows that God works through whomsoever He chooses, laying long-term plans, drawing us to Him even through our weakness so we may later collaborate with Him powerfully for the redemption of souls. As Queen, Bathsheba saves the day for everyone; much more does Mary.

Next we turn our thoughts to the Spouse of the Blessed Virgin Mary, St Joseph. We discover that his relation to Mary is subtly indicated in the successive lives of the four women of the previous section. And we examine how he is undeniably prefigured by the ancient Patriarch Joseph. This is important for its own sake and because in recognising the OT includes prefigurations of St Joseph, all the more can we expect to find Mary also prefigured and, with certainty, Jesus Christ.

Finally, the last section, *Memorare*, offers reasons why understanding such prefigurations, and loving them, is a vital defence against the assaults of hell.

THE TRIUMPH OF MARY'S IMMACULATE HEART

A vision of hell was given on 13th July 1917 by the Virgin Mary to three shepherd children at Fatima. Our Lady explained that great trials faced the Church but assured her little children that, whatever course the final persecution took, "in the end, my Immaculate Heart will triumph". Reading the Bible in the light of this heavenly promise, and discovering the same message hidden in multiple stories, we grow in confident expectation of her victory.

When the end approaches:

> *there will be a great tribulation, such as has not been from the beginning of the world until the present, and such as will not be. And unless those days had been shortened, no flesh would be saved. But for the sake of the elect, those days shall be shortened. Then if anyone will have said to you, 'Behold, here is the Christ,' or 'he is there,' do not be willing to believe it. For there will arise false Christs and false prophets. And they will produce great signs and wonders, so much so as to lead into error even the elect (if this could be). Behold, I have warned you beforehand.* (Mt 24:21-25)

Jesus says He has warned us *"beforehand"*. The Word of God did this not only here in the Gospel, but throughout the OT. God knows it will be hard for us to hold our spiritual nerve when the days are darkest. Jesus implies it will be impossible to be saved in the last days except for those who heed His teaching, who know in advance to reject the *"false Christs and false prophets"*, not deceived by their *"great signs and wonders"*. The stories of the twelve women (Eve plus the seven, then the additional four) and Mary as their fulfilment arm us for this combat. They tell us not to stand back as spectators but to imitate our Queen in prayer and fasting and to be proactive in overcoming our enemies. This is not a matter for the last days alone but for every soul. Our lives contribute either to the building up of the City of God or else of its opponent, the City of Man.

This corporate responsibility is unmissable in the OT accounts examined below, which make clear that by detesting sin we can help save others beside ourselves. Variously the heroines indicate the importance of our energetic exertion defending against the unholy, or of wisdom in politics, or of courage and purity, even the readiness to lose one's life for God, offering it in total immolation, anticipating Mary's mystical martyrdom on Calvary. Evil has no victory in such souls, who

> *overcame the accuser by the blood of the Lamb and by the word of His testimony. And they loved not their own lives, even unto death.* (Apoc 12:11)

The *"accuser"* here is satan. The ancient serpent is opposed to the Woman and seeks to devour her offspring (Apoc 12:17). satan's servants and acolytes on earth pursue this purpose on his behalf, there being many of them, the worst ones being corrupt clerics emerging from the Church herself, wolves in sheep's clothing. St John wrote:

And, as you have heard that the Antichrist is coming, so now many antichrists have arrived. By this, we know that it is the last hour. They went out from among us, but they were not of us... (1 Jn 2:18-19)[2]

Not all evil men are antichrists, but those are who seek to build a following among men in explicitly opposing the Holy Trinity, denying Jesus is the Son of God, refusing to acknowledge He is the Christ, the Messiah.

Who is a liar, other than he who denies that Jesus is the Christ? This one is the Antichrist, who denies the Father and the Son. (1 Jn 2:22)

The last Antichrist will be the worst. He will be a man, possibly of Dan (any non-Jews claiming to be the Messiah will struggle to get traction). His agenda will be served by all *"the merchants of the earth"* (Apoc 18:2-23), that is through the love of money (1 Tim 6:10). Mammon ensnares men so that they cannot serve God (Mt 6:24). The greed of every generation, all frivolous buying, deceitful selling and avaricious hoarding, is building up toward this until, finally, the world's usurious system of finance collapses in a *"single hour"*, that is, a colossal crash (Apoc 18:10,17,19).

This process of monetary hegemony is twinned with every political machination through history which has strained toward an unbalanced accumulation of power, every tyranny

---

2 Where "Antichrist" is capitalised, it refers to the last one. Where it is lower case, it refers to the forerunners. And although in this work "Lucifer" is capitalised according to convention, I prefer not to capitalise satan. Better to signal to him that his head is crushed, hence the lower case.

and cabal which advances a single world order, which seeks global domination. This ruthless regime is figured by the sea beast (Apoc 13:1-10).

The totalitarian plexus in politics and finance will collaborate with the Antichrist as he introduces his false religion. This corrupt religion, arising from Israel, is figured by the land beast (Apoc 13:11-18).[3] A key collaborator will be the *"false prophet"* (Apoc 16:13), a deceiving religious persona who disorientates through wicked wonders.

Once established, the Antichrist will compel all men to worship him or face death. The saints will not comply. He will claim to be the Messiah, the promised Christ, which no faithful Christian can accept.[4] This is not a matter for the future alone. Though we do not know if the end will come in two thousand years, or two hundred, or twenty, the point is that it is underway now. We need to choose sides now. St John writes to us:

Every spirit who confesses that Jesus Christ has arrived in the Flesh is of God; and every spirit who contradicts Jesus is not of God. And this one is the Antichrist, the

---

[3] The Gentiles are represented biblically by the islands or the seas, being isolated or unstable (Gen 10:5; Ps 72:10; 143:7; Is 17:12; Zeph 2:11; Apoc 17:15). In contrast, "earth" or "land" often refers to Israel as either the people or the Holy Land (being solidly grounded in God and founded on His promises), and thereby also to the Church and even Heaven (Lev 25:23; Dt 9:4-6; Jer 22:29; Amos 7:17; Heb 4:1-3).

[4] St Irenæus, *Adversus Haereses*, V, 25, 1-5, The Antichrist, "being an apostate and a robber, is anxious to be adored as God. [In] the temple in Jerusalem… the enemy shall sit, endeavouring to show himself as Christ… When he comes, he shall reign over the earth… shall sit in the temple of God, leading astray those who worship him, as if he were Christ."

*one that you have heard is coming, and even now he is
in the world.* (1 Jn 4:2-3)

The antichrist is in the world now by way of anticipation in
the lives of those who, abusing their great talents and high
calling, rebel satanically against the Almighty. Refusing to
honour Him, they desire unlawful dominion, crushing others
in order to control them. They use bribery, lies and murder to
'succeed'. Only the most wicked among them understand
what a tower of hell they are building, but they are as
committed to it as were in ancient days the Tower of Babel's
builders (Gen 11:1-9).

Admittedly, in the OT we think not of *"antichrists"*, not of
men who claim to be Christ before He actually came, not of
men who deny *"the Father and the Son"*, before the Holy
Trinity had even been revealed. But the antichrists are
prefigured in the OT, as indicated in the Epistle of St Jude
(Jud 4*ff*). They are lovers of themselves, stealing power to
subjugate others, enemies of God's people, conspiring to take
for themselves what belongs to God, ultimately the place of
His worship:

*O God, who shall be like to thee? Hold not thy peace,
neither be thou still, O God. For lo, thy enemies have
[sounded off]: and they that hate thee have lifted up
[their] head. They have taken a malicious counsel
against thy people, and have consulted against thy
saints. They have said: Come and let us destroy them, so
that they be not a nation: and let the name of Israel be*

remembered no more. For they have contrived with one consent: they have made a covenant together against thee... Do to them as thou didst to Madian and to Sisara: as to Jabin at the brook of Cisson. Who perished at Endor: and became as dung for the earth... All their princes, who have said: 'Let us possess the sanctuary of God for an inheritance.' (Ps 82:2-13 DRB)

This Psalm begins: *"O God, who shall be like to thee?"* The Archangel Michael's very name proclaims this question (מִיכָאֵל, *Quis ut Deus?*). To him it is given to defeat those who ask the question in pride rather than in adoration. St Michael's very name drives satan out from the heavens and casts him into the abyss (Apoc 12:7-9; 20:3).

On earth it is given to the saints to participate in this warfare — to overcome the antichrists. The Psalm above cries out: *"they that hate thee have lifted up their head"*. But they lifted it only for it to be crushed, as the same Psalm alludes to the pitiful fate of Sisera. It was Jael who broke his skull with a hammer blow. We are to do similarly. We are to reject satan, and all his pomps and works, to permit him no part in us, to refuse his seductions to sin. This includes to reject his agents on earth, his antichrists, who deny the Blessed Trinity and the Incarnation, denying *"the Flesh"* and the Real Presence of Our Lord in the Holy Eucharist. If we allow them no sway in our souls, then we have crushed the serpent's head. The Magnificat Antiphon for the Feasts of Apostles encourages us: "Be valiant in battle, fight the ancient serpent and accept the eternal kingdom. Alleluia."

How shall we engage in this battle? We have help from our heavenly Mother. Mary gave birth to Jesus. She gives birth also to us. The baptised are the members of Christ's Body. Mary is our spiritual Mother. Pope St Pius X taught that Mary is the channel, or "neck", who connects all members with Jesus.[5] As with a natural birth, first to be born is the head; so we may say the last generation to be born will be as heel and foot. It will fall to them finally to crush the serpent's head. They will achieve this, it seems, through a total devotion to Jesus through Mary. That is, Mary and Jesus achieving it in them.

Throughout Sacred Scripture, God is intoning for us a most earnest poem, a poem in which it is not the lines which rhyme but the events, a poem structured not in strophes but in saints, and in which every verse speaks somehow of Christ. These women of the OT have much to say about the Mother of Christ. At least a dozen of them, including Eve our first mother, tell of Mary's victory over the Antichrist. This is well worth exploring.

---

[5] Pope St Pius X, *Ad diem illum lætissimum*, 13, "Mary, as St. Bernard justly remarks, is the channel; or, if you will, the connecting portion the function of which is to join the Body to the head and to transmit to the body the influences and volitions of the head — We mean the neck. Yes, says St. Bernardine of Sienna, 'she is the neck of Our Head, by which He communicates to His mystical body all spiritual gifts'."

THE WOMAN: PROMISED IN PARADISE

And the Lord God said to the serpent: '...I will put enmities between you and the woman, between your offspring and her offspring. She will crush your head, and you will lie in wait for her heel.'

— Gen 3:14-15

While Adam and Eve were sinking in the distress of being caught in their sin, God announced perpetual enmity between the serpent and *"the woman"*, and between the serpent's offspring and her offspring (Gen 3:14-15). This *"woman"* is the Blessed Virgin Mary. Her offspring is Jesus Christ. But is it He, or is it she, who crushes satan's head?

The Vulgate (Latin), translated by St Jerome, has *"she"* (*ipsa*) in Gen 3:15.[6] The Septuagint (Greek) has *"he"* (αὐτός). The Hebrew sources are mixed, with some manuscripts and historical commentators reading *"he"* and others *"she"*.[7] Arguments over centuries attempting to settle the matter have become formidably technical and even heated.

---

[6] The Neo-Vulgate has *"it"* (*ipsum*), referring to her *"offspring"* or *"seed"* (*semen*), which is neuter in Latin.

[7] The earliest forms of written Hebrew do not distinguish between *"he"* and *"she"*. Both appear as הוא . The script developed after Moses wrote the Torah, so that from the Book of Joshua onwards one can distinguish *"she"* (היא as used in Josh 2:6) from *"he"* (הוא as in Josh 3:1), the second letter being respectively a Yod or a Vav. About one thousand years after Christ, vowels were added to the entire Tanakh, enabling distinctions to be made in the Torah between *"she"* (הִוא as used for Eve in Gen 3:12), and *"he"* (הוּא as used for Adam in Gen 3:16).

Whatever the difficulties with the text, the Church's magisterial interpretation in the light of the whole of Revelation has been attested by numerous saints, Fathers, scholastic doctors and popes of two millennia. A definitive summing up came on 8th December 1854 when Pope Pius IX declared the Dogma of the Immaculate Conception. Here the Church rejoices in Jesus Christ as the unique and absolute Redeemer of mankind, and exults also in the Virgin Mary as "the all fair and immaculate one who has crushed the poisonous head of the most cruel serpent..."[8]

Jesus and Mary acting together in crushing the serpent's head was depicted in the painting of Caravaggio (✝1610), *Madonna dei Palafrenieri*, long before the definition of the Immaculate Conception (1854). Clearly this understanding was broadly received in the Church. The painting shows Jesus acting through Mary. Jesus is calm; Mary is maternal. Crushing satan is child's play. These aspects are vital truths for the triumph of Mary's Immaculate Heart and Jesus' Sacred Heart. He touches His Heart with one hand, stretching out the other, heralding His Crucifixion. There is significance too in the presence of St Anne if she may be taken to represent harmonious support of the OT.

Evidently, to accept both readings of *"he"* and *"she"* as communicating truth is not merely a diplomatic compromise, nor simply a realistic recognition of the ambiguity of the sources. It is a theological acclamation of Jesus acting in Mary

---

[8] Pope Pius IX, *Ineffabilis Deus*, 8th Dec 1854, "the most holy Virgin, united with [Jesus] by a most intimate and indissoluble bond, was, with Him and through Him, eternally at enmity with the evil serpent, and most completely triumphed over him, and thus crushed his head with her immaculate foot."

and Mary in Jesus — a kind of circumincession of their souls, or perfect harmony of intellect, will and emotions. Aspects of this intimacy are described by St Louis Marie de Montfort in his *True Devotion to Mary*.

Though humans have disagreed over the interpretation of Gen 3:15, our confusion is mild in comparison with that of the devil. He understood the sentence included *"she"*. He was there! God spoke to him. His perplexity lay in trying to grasp how on earth, how in the whole of creation, could a woman, a human, crush his heinous head? And which woman?

There is a backstory. In the beginning Lucifer was the prince of all angels, the mightiest, the most intelligent, the one with the strongest will.[9] He was created with surpassing honours. He did not envy God, for all angels know God is Eternal Being, the Only Almighty, their Creator.[10] However, God put all the angels to a test before revealing His own inner life to them, or rather, before revealing his Trinitarian identity to those who would pass the test. The Church does not teach definitively in what this test consisted but the best theologians

---

[9] St Thomas, *S.Th.* I, Q.63 a.7, cites Pope St Gregory the Great saying "the chief angel who sinned, 'being set over all the hosts of angels, surpassed them in brightness, and was by comparison the most illustrious among them.'"

St Bonaventure, *II Sent.* d.VI a.1 q.1, concludes Lucifer was pre-eminent among the angels and of the highest angelic order.

[10] St Thomas, *S.Th.* I, Q.63 a.3, "[The devil] could not seek to be as God [by equality]; because by natural knowledge he knew that this was impossible... it is impossible for one angel of lower degree to desire equality with a higher; and still more to covet equality with God." Also *S.C.G.* III, q.109, n.8 "not that [the devil's] good might be equal to the divine good, because such a thing could not come into his mind." And *De malo*, q.16, a.3 "the devil's will could not have inclined to desire equality with God absolutely."

deduce God showed them something about the economy of salvation. The angels who freely accepted God's Plan immediately gained the beatific vision to enjoy for eternity. Those who rejected it were damned irrevocably to hell.[11]

Whatever the test was, Lucifer was appalled by it. Franciscan tradition relates that the angels apprehended God's decree that an infant boy in the arms of his mother would rise to be King of Heaven and she to be Queen, to whom all other creatures were subject. Lucifer could not freely accept that an animal, albeit rational, that is human (*homo sapiens / animal rationale*) would reign even over him.[12] This provoked his narcissistic fury. He rebelled: *"non serviam!"*[13] In that moment, hell came into existence: a state of irretrievable separation from God. A third of the spirits fell with Lucifer, to be named angels no more but demons. Driven by self-destructive hate, they work ceaselessly to separate humans from God.

---

[11] St Augustine, *De Civitate dei*, XI, 33, "That certain angels sinned, and were thrust down to the lowest parts of this world, where they are, as it were, incarcerated till their final damnation in the day of judgment, the Apostle Peter very plainly declares, when he says that *'For God did not spare those angels who sinned, but instead delivered them, as if dragged down by infernal ropes, into the torments of the underworld, to be reserved unto judgment'* (2 Pet 2:4)..."

See also St Thomas, *S.Th.* I, Q.63 a.4.

[12] St Thomas, *S.Th.* I, Q.63 a.2, "the wicked angel... coveted a singular excellence, which would cease to be singular because of the excellence of some other."

St Bonaventure, *II Sent.* d.XXI a.1 q.1, explains that in pride the devil wanted to dominate men as if he were himself God, and in envy sought to prevent men enjoying the blessedness which he had forfeited.

[13] *"From ancient times, you have broken my yoke... you have said, 'I will not serve'"* (Jer 2:20). This rebellion against God began with Lucifer. According to Tertullian, *De patientiæ*, V, the devil could not bear "that the Lord God subjected the universal works which He had made to His own image, that is, to man."

What could satan do? The following few pages, heavily footnoted, speculate on his mindset.

satan resented Adam and Eve walking through Eden in friendship with God. Were these the man and the woman who would rise above him?[14] The man had been commanded by God not to eat the fruit of the tree of knowledge. The woman was not present when the command was given; she only heard it from her husband. It would be easier to draw her away from him than to draw him away from God. The devil tempted her, and she ate. She tempted her husband, and he ate. Thus, through *"the envy of the devil, death entered the world"* (Wis 2:24).

satan saw he had successfully sown devastating mistrust between man and woman. Better still, he had robbed Adam of friendship with God. That meant all Adam's descendants would be denied this precious inheritance.[15] Nothing on earth could perfectly unite human beings again. Best of all, they

---

[14] Whereas St Ambrose, St Anselm and St Thomas favoured the teaching that God became incarnate in order to redeem man from sin, Bl Duns Scotus took the position that God would have become incarnate whether or not man sinned. He taught that God's very first decree in relation to Creation was the universal primacy of Jesus Christ. The Virgin Mary, as Jesus' Mother, is raised by the fullness of grace above all other creatures. All this is prior to sin or redemption. Followers of Scotus speculated that the specific realisation that a woman would be Queen of Angels provoked Lucifer to rebel. He might have willingly bowed to God made Man (though it is not sure he knew this profundity in God's Plan), but he was not willing to serve a human creature, given humans were by nature lower than angels (cf. Ps 8:6). The devil's refusal to freely subject himself to the Woman is made explicit in the works of the Venerable Mary of Ágreda and St Maximilian Kolbe.

[15] Pope St Leo I, *Letter to Flavian, Bishop of Constantinople*, "It was the devil's boast that humanity had been deceived by his trickery and so had lost the gifts God had given it; and that it had been stripped of the endowment of immortality and so was subject to the harsh sentence of death." According to Pope St Leo, the devil had failed to perceive God's deeper plan of redemption.

would be separated from God for eternity. Every single one of them damned! How could any human rise above him now?

Then came God's announcement. Directly the Lord God said to the serpent:

> *Because you have done this, you are cursed among all living things, even the wild beasts of the earth. Upon your breast shall you travel, and the ground shall you eat, all the days of your life. I will put enmities between you and the woman, between your offspring and her offspring. She will crush your head, and you will lie in wait for her heel.* (Gen 3:14-15)

The devil knew God's Word is true, but he could not see how.[16] How could a woman harm him? He had seen how weak women were. Why should he care if her seed were opposed to his? He had seen how weak men were. And was one of these supposed to crush his head? He could not see it.[17] But he knew it was true, causing him perpetual angst. In futility he sought to understand it.

---

[16] The devil, the first liar, knows God speaks only the truth, that He "can neither deceive nor be deceived" (Vatican I, *Dei Filius,* 3).

[17] St Thomas, *S.Th.* I, Q.64 a.1, expounds on the limited knowledge of the demons: "Dionysius says, 'certain gifts were bestowed upon the demons which, we say, have not been changed at all, but remain entire and most brilliant' (*Div. Nom.* iv). Now, the knowledge of truth stands among those natural gifts... Consequently their natural knowledge was not diminished. The second kind of knowledge... which comes of grace, and consists in speculation, has not been utterly taken away from them, but lessened; ...of Divine secrets only so much is revealed to them as is necessary... but not in the same degree as to the holy angels, to whom many more things are revealed, and more fully, in the Word Himself. But of the third knowledge [the gift of wisdom which produces] charity, they are utterly deprived."

Meanwhile, he noticed encouraging developments. While Adam and Eve were torn with sorrow, Cain copied satan's own envy and slew his brother. What pleased satan most was not simply seeing Cain confounded and made a fugitive on earth; even better was that the just Abel did not enter into Heaven, but was stuck in Limbo.[18]

In the generations that followed, the devil's satisfaction solidified. Besides countless thieves, perverts, murderers and idolators being condemned in their sin, even the God-fearing Seth, Methuselah and Abraham (Abraham!) were locked in death — all of them. Well, it was true that one or two escaped his bookkeeping: that man Enoch, and the prophet Elijah, he did not know what became of them. But the scoreline was overwhelmingly in satan's favour.

However, those words of God troubled him. They were true. And every now and then he noticed his protégés having their heads crushed by a woman. This troubled him to the core.[19] There was Jael; and that woman who smashed a grinding stone on the head of his servant Abimelech; and, worst of all, that fearless Judith. How he hated her — her prayers, her fasting, her chastity, her prudence, her total trust in God. If satan had a spine, then Judith hacking off

---

[18] Before Christ opened Heaven, the *limbus patrum*, or Limbo of the Fathers, was where souls of the just went after their death. Jesus referred to it as the *"bosom of Abraham"* (Lk 16:22). Jesus opened Heaven with His Ascension, thereby emptying Limbo as its population entered into the beatific vision.

[19] St Augustine, *De Civitate Dei*, XI, 33, writes of the fallen angels "swelling with pride... reeking with the unclean lust of self-advancement... raging through the lower regions of the air... tempest-tossed with beclouding desires... boiling with the lust of subduing and hurting..."

Holofernes' head would have sent shivers down it. But even she, when she died, was trapped by death and remained separated from God.

In the fullness of time, satan suffered a scare. There was a man named John in the desert, dressed in camel skins, who ate mostly locusts and honey. He was so simple, so strong, so holy: he did not seem ever to sin. And preaching he became phenomenally popular. Half the world went to him for baptism. Was this the promised Messiah?[20] John himself denied it: *"non sum ego Christus"* (Jn 1:20). How could he be the threatened seed of the woman anyway? His mother Elizabeth was holy all right, but having already died, she posed no threat. Then John himself was beheaded and not even he who committed no offence was able to enter Heaven. That original sin was powerful! If someone as great as John could not enter the so-called Kingdom, then surely God would be isolated forever.

But satan knew God's Word is true. So he could not rest. *"You believe that there is one God. You do well. The demons also believe, and they tremble greatly"* (Jas 2:19). That Protoevangelium ('first gospel') of Gen 3:15, such a comfort to mankind, was pure frustration to the devil's intellect and

---

[20] St Thomas, *II Sent.,* d.XI q.2 a.4, teaches that the good angels knew in substance of the Incarnation and Passion and Resurrection of Christ from the beginning of time, but did not know of exactly when or how it would be fulfilled until it happened. It is probable that the fallen angels did not even know of the substance of these mysteries until they were openly revealed.

torment to his pride.[21] Before being beheaded, John had baptised his cousin, Jesus. Was Jesus the Messiah?[22]

The devil tried tempting Him in the desert, without success. Jesus was sharper and more resilient than Job! Though John's popularity was great, it did not compare to this Man's. satan sent his earthly agents to watch Jesus, to catch Him out in hard questions, to trap Him with snares. But he could not lay a ghostly finger on Him. And this Jesus, He thundered against satan's own spawn:

> *You are of your father, the devil. And you will carry out the desires of your father. He was a murderer from the beginning. And he did not stand in the truth, because the truth is not in him. When he speaks a lie, he speaks it from his own self. For he is a liar, and the father of lies.* (Jn 8:44)

---

[21] St Augustine, *De Civitate Dei*, XIV, 3, "We cannot call the devil a fornicator or drunkard… yet he is exceedingly proud and envious. [For] who shows more hatred to the saints? Who is more at variance with them? Who more envious, bitter, and jealous?"

[22] Some of the demons knew Jesus was the Messiah: *"What are we to you, Jesus of Nazareth? Have you come to destroy us? I know who you are: the Holy One of God"* (Lk 4:34). Others even said: *"You are the Son of God"* (Mk 3:12; cf. Mt 8:29). Jesus commanded all these to silence so that they could not announce this to men prematurely and possibly prohibited communication among the demons. Before this satan seems unsure, repeatedly asking, *"If you are the Son of God…"* (Mt 4:3,6; Lk 4:3,9). St Thomas, *S.Th.* III, Q.47 a.5, citing the C.4th *Quaestiones Veteris et Novi Testamenti*, Q.LXVI, writes that the Jewish "elders, who were called 'rulers, knew,' as did also the devils, 'that He was the Christ promised in the Law: for they saw all the signs in Him which the prophets said would come to pass: but they did not know the mystery of His Godhead'."

Here was enmity! This teaching had to stop or all Israel would follow Him. Expert in the Scriptures, satan did not want to risk the Jews attaining unity through holiness. He had already seen how prophets like Elijah and Jeremiah confounded his lies; how kings like Hezekiah and Josiah salvaged order from his sacrilegious chaos; how priests like Zadok and Ezra spread sanctity among the people. The devil did not want this Jesus of Nazareth to rise as prophet; or king; or priest.

Though few others realised, it had not escaped satan's observation that Jesus was the last in the direct line of King David. It was highly unusual that Jesus had not married even by the age of thirty. If satan could get Him killed before He had children, would that not confound God's promise of an everlasting throne to David's offspring?

So satan sowed a murderous hatred against Jesus among the elders. Next he entered into one of Jesus' disciples, one of His inner circle, and had him betray His Master.[23] It was hard work, but satan managed to capitalise on centuries of corruption in the Sanhedrin and High Priesthood to have them condemn Jesus without cause. Through these he manipulated the whole city to call out, *"crucify Him"*.[24] Pilate was difficult. He kept trying to release Jesus. It was the fault, thought satan, of Pilate's wife. Insufferable woman, for she seduced her husband toward justice. But ambition had raised

---

[23] See Jn 13:27. Of Judas it was written one thousand years beforehand: *"Set thou the sinner over him: and may the devil stand at his right hand"* (Ps 108:6 DRB).

[24] For the miserable corruption of the High Priesthood under Jason and Menelaus two hundred years before the Crucifixion, see 2 Macc 4:1-50. For its lamentable end with Phannias ben Samuel in 70 A.D., see Josephus, *Jewish Wars*, Bk IV, 3.

Pilate to a position requiring a moral strength he did not have. The governor was already afraid of having his record ruined by riots in Jerusalem (Mt 27:24), and now team satan threatened his reputation for loyalty to Caesar (Jn 19:12). That was enough to break Pilate.

So the King of the Jews was led away to be crucified. He was nailed onto a Cross on Calvary. His Mother just stood there. She was a quiet one. As Jesus bled to death, with every drop of Blood that fell, satan's confidence in himself waxed high: if he could stop this Man's ministry, and remove Him from the face of the earth, what could he not achieve?

The devil did not have to wait until the Resurrection to realise he had lost all. Immediately when Jesus died, satan saw this One could not be stopped.[25] Jesus was fully active. In power He came and comforted myriads of souls in the prison of death. With absolute clarity, Jesus preached His Gospel in Sheol (Jn 5:25,28; 1 Pet 3:19). Truth routed lies. The light shone in the darkness, words far brighter than photons, like billions of unstoppable swords. The darkness was defenceless.

Now satan knew, in his vast intelligence, that here was One infinitely stronger than Adam. He perceived that the place of the Crucifixion was Eden. Mary was the New Eve. Her Son was God's Son, a Divine Person. Such a love had never entered satan's mind. That God would take Flesh from a creature, and then the Strong One surrender what he had

---

[25] St Ignatius of Antioch, *Epistle to the Ephesians*, XIX, "Now the virginity of Mary was hidden from the prince of this world, as was also her offspring, and the death of the Lord; three mysteries of renown, which were wrought in silence by God."

taken, letting Himself be cruelly killed! Who could have guessed? Well, this unnoticeable lady, Mary, had seen it coming. And Jesus, by His Resurrection and Ascension, opened up Heaven to the righteous, stripping satan of all his valuable plunder. The souls remaining to fill hell were the rotten ones, stinking, hateful, arrogant — hardly a prize.

His pride crucified, satan knew he had been defeated not by God only but also by a woman. Not simply through her singular privilege of being immaculately conceived, which was entirely God's work, but deservedly, meritoriously, by her lifetime of cooperation with God. For though he had never succeeded in tempting her into sin, finally satan saw at the death of her Son that never would he be able to do so. Under the most piercing agony of heart which any human being could suffer, the Mother of God did not breathe a word of hatred against her Son's enemies, nor for a moment despair of God's Goodness, nor for a second hold back anything of herself from Him. Mary stood and faced the whole Sacrifice and freely offered her beloved Son. Here was the perpetual enmity between the serpent and the woman which God had announced in Eden: the enmity was absolute, uninterrupted — not once had satan managed to subjugate Mary to sin.

And satan feared the future victory of the Mother of God. He remembered Jael and Esther and Susanna, and understood. He realised that Mary, the Immaculate Conception, would crush his head. Though he would rage desperately throughout the rest of history (Apoc 12:12), by this he serves to make holy souls holier still and the company of hell more detestable.

"Non serviam!" he had sworn, but he could not escape from serving God's purpose. He knew he must lose. He knew that for every soul he dragged to hell his own eternal punishment would increase accordingly. Yet he would not relent in his attacks, being driven by a hatred so strong it overrode the warnings of his own intelligence.[26] Hopelessly, he will continue until the final crushing of his head.

To speculate further, what or who is the serpent's head? In the garden satan spoke through a snake, but he himself is a fallen angel, not an animal. He is unable to take on flesh. His *"head"* is not part of his body, for he has none. Is it the chief of his embodied (human) followers?[27] Unlike Jesus Christ, Who unites His saints as members of His Mystical Body, there is no equivalent body for satan. He ceaselessly sows division, so even those who follow him are disunited. In contrast, the Members of Christ work together by the sap of grace. Jesus is the tree of the first Psalm, planted beside living waters, yielding fruit in its seasons, whose leaf will not fall away. But *"Not so the impious, not so. For they are like the dust that the*

---

[26] Angels, good or bad, do not make intellectual mistakes (although they can have blind spots in their knowledge). Consequently angels, good or bad, never change their mind. Those who, with disordered priorities knowingly chose damnation over honouring the Woman, will never repent of it. This is the mystery of iniquity. It cannot be fathomed.

[27] St Augustine, *On Christian Doctrine*, III, 37, "When Scripture speaks of one and the same person, [we] take pains to understand which part of the statement applies to the head and which to the body... statements are sometimes made about the devil, whose truth is not so evident in regard to himself as in regard to his body... For, although the devil sends his angels to all nations, yet it is his body, not himself, that is ground down on the earth, except that he himself is in his body, which is beaten small like the dust which the wind blows from the face of the earth."

wind casts along the face of the earth" (Ps 1:4). Acolytes of satan are not bound together in a body, but are dispersed like parched dust, devoured by him but not assimilated: *"cursed are you... upon your belly you shall go, and dust you shall eat all the days of your life"* (Gen 3:14 RSVCE).

What of the head, though? The devil tries to ape the Church. Christ, Who is the Head of the Church, has a vicar as His representative. That is, the pope is the visible head of Christ's Body on earth. The orderly succession of popes through the centuries makes the unity of the Body clear. Meanwhile, *"many antichrists have come"* (1 Jn 2:18), *"those who do not confess that Jesus Christ has arrived in the flesh. Such a one as this is a deceiver and an antichrist"* (2 Jn 7). These *"many deceivers"* are not continuous, but disjointed, even opposed to each other — Marcion, Mohammed, Luther, Marx, Mao. Yet they are preparing the way for the most evil human being ever, one who will be fully aware of his servitude to satan. In this limited sense, we may regard the Antichrist as satan's 'head' on earth. Our Lady will crush him.

How will this happen? Mary is not going to return bodily to earth. Rather St Louis Marie de Montfort predicts that those dedicated to God through her, devoted by a holy slavery of love to Jesus through Mary, will be the saints who, amid many martyrs, withstand the persecution of the Antichrist and overcome, until the point is reached when evil irretrievably devours itself. It will be Mary who triumphs totally as flawless example for these saints, as patient teacher of their virtues, as ever active Mother who protects, as holy Queen of

Heaven who reigns, as unique channel of grace and as true guide toward her Son. It will be a spiritual victory, manifested in the world for all to see.

God does not mean to leave us in the dark but to illumine us. That which God first promised in the Protoevangelium, He repeats again and again throughout the Bible so as to keep our hope lively. He feeds us with new details and vantage points to help our understanding. We turn our attention now to these veiled but vital assurances.

JAEL: CRUSHING THE ENEMY'S TEMPLE

And so Jael, the wife of Heber, took a spike from the tent, and also took a mallet. And entering unseen and with silence, she placed the spike over the temple of his head. And striking it with the mallet, she drove it through his brain, as far as the ground. And so, joining deep sleep to death, he fell unconscious and died. And behold, Barak arrived, in pursuit of Sisera. And Jael, going out to meet him, said to him, 'Come, and I will show you the man whom you are seeking.' And when he had entered her tent, he saw Sisera lying dead, with the spike fixed in his temples.

— Jdg 4:21-22

The first time one reads of Jael crushing Sisera's head, one might or might not recall God's decree that the woman would crush the serpent's head. Yet the more one investigates Jael's graphic story (Jdg 4-5), the more details one discovers which make the connection impossible to deny. Ultimately, this is all about Mary defeating the Antichrist.

The story is presented twice: once as narrative (Jdg 4), then commemorated in Deborah's Song (Jdg 5). The second version has a tone of great celebration and is given a deeper historical context. So we may see a parallel with Our Lady's victory being won on earth in history, and afterwards celebrated forever in Heaven; or being first alluded to in Genesis, and finally in the Apocalypse.

The momentous battle which Jael's action completes takes place near Megiddo (Jdg 5:19), which is none other than Armageddon, the place the Apocalypse identifies for the final battle.[28] Prophetically, Deborah's Song attributes a cosmic significance to the fight:

> *The conflict against [the kings of Canaan] was from heaven. The stars, remaining in their order and courses, fought against Sisera. The torrent of Kishon dragged away their carcasses, the onrushing torrent, the torrent of Kishon. O my soul, tread upon the stalwart!* (Jdg 5:20-21)

Deborah rejoices that heaven fights for the Israelites. The stars which remain in their courses represent the angels who did not fall (Apoc 12:4,9). Since Jesus opened Heaven, the stars also represent the saints (1 Cor 15:41-42), governed by the twelve Apostles who crown Our Lady (Apoc 12:1). Their combined love is forceful and ebullient as the torrent which dragged away the defeated enemies so their carcasses were swallowed up by the sea, that is, hell.

"O my soul, tread upon the stalwart!" Tread upon the mighty of this world, the powerful oppressor. In Greek the word is δυνατός, of whom Mary sang in her Magnificat that God *"has deposed the powerful from their seat"* (Lk 1:52). What an emotional surge, a spiritual joy, to see the unjust deposed. We love it in every movie, to see evil defeated, the

---

[28] *"And he shall gather them together at a place which is called, in Hebrew, Armageddon. And the seventh Angel poured out his bowl upon the air. And a great voice went out of the temple from the throne, saying: 'It is done'"* (Apoc 16:16-17).

humble surmounting; much more in real life; and above all, in the final confrontation. *"O Lord,"* sang Deborah, *"so may all your enemies perish! But may those who love you shine with splendour, as the sun shines at its rising"* (Jdg 5:31). Here the successful battle against Jabin's general, Sisera, gives us a foretaste of how all God's enemies perish, including at the very end. But those who love God will *"shine with splendour, as the sun shines at its rising"*, which means the general Resurrection, when the saints will be glorified in Christ.

The background to the battle is that God had rescued His People many times by raising up wise and mighty judges to lead them. Heaven worked through the hearts of men to bring change on earth and to give God's People rest from their enemies. Even so:

> *the sons of Israel resumed doing evil in the sight of the Lord. And the Lord delivered them into the hands of Jabin, the king of Canaan.* (Jdg 4:1-2)

It is exasperating to read how often Israel was unfaithful. It is more uncomfortable still to make an examination of conscience and see we are no better. It is a forewarning, for those who care, of the great apostasy in the Church, wherein the hearts of many grow cold and Christians will be given into the hands of their enemies (2 Thes 2:3; Mt 24:12; Apoc 13:7). A massive turning away from God is underway today. Aleksandr Solzhenitsyn admonished, "man has forgotten God".[29] Who knows if for the final time?

---

[29] Aleksandr Solzhenitsyn, *Templeton Prize Acceptance Address*, 10th May 1983.

In Deborah's day the enemy was a remote king who sent a vicious general with his army to crush Israel. Interpreted, satan is the prince who remains at a distance while operating through his chief agent on earth, the Antichrist. Likewise we do not see satan, but nations suffer disorientation and exspoliation at the hands of his human abettors. In this study:

> *Jabin, the king of Canaan reigned at Hazor. And he had a commander of his army named Sisera, but this man lived at Harosheth of the Gentiles. And the sons of Israel cried out to the Lord. For he had nine hundred chariots with scythes, and he vehemently oppressed them for twenty years.* (Jdg 4:2-3)

Harosheth of the Gentiles is in Galilee, not far from Nazareth. It was a cosmopolitan area, which indicates in Jesus His love for all peoples.[30] But in Sisera, who represents the Antichrist, it hints at globalism, at massive messianic claims. Portentously, Sisera's weapons involved cruel technology (*"nine hundred chariots with scythes"*) and he used them to effect, vehemently oppressing the sons of Israel.

Not all the Israelis were willing to fight. Deborah sings that the Reubenites were incapacitated by infighting, Manasseh had drifted away, Dan was preoccupied with trade, Asher with depravity.[31] But an Israeli army was raised, ten thousand in

---

[30] "Cosmopolitan" derives from κόσμος ("universe") and πολίτης (one "of a city"), rendering the idea of a universal city, or citizenship of the world, all peoples united.

[31] Interpreting: *"Reuben was divided against himself. Contention was found among great souls. Gilead rested beyond the Jordan, and Dan was occupied with ships. Asher was living on the shore of the sea, and dwelling in the ports"* (Jdg 5:17).

number and formidable in courage, for *"truly, Zebulun and Naphtali offered their lives to death"* (Jdg 5:18; cf. Jdg 4:10). These are at the heart of Galilee, true Galileans we might say, present to fight when it matters. We may think of the Apostles (Mt 4:13-22; Is 9:1-2).

The army's leader, *"Barak, the son of Abinoam, had ascended to Mount Tabor"* (Jdg 4:12). This is where Jesus would be transfigured in a cloud with His saints and was revealed to His disciples in blinding glory (Mt 17:1-9). So we may think of Jesus on the Last Day, *"coming on a cloud, with great power and glory"* (Lk 21:27), when we read:

> *And Deborah said to Barak: 'Rise up. For this is the day on which the Lord delivers Sisera into your hands. For [the Lord] is your commander.' And so, Barak descended from Mount Tabor, and the ten thousand fighting men with him.* (Jdg 4:14)

Glorious! Fear of the Lord puts the enemy to rout; their general, Sisera, flees on foot and his entire army is annihilated (Jdg 4:15-16). Sisera seeks refuge among those he thinks are friends, the house of Heber the Kenite (Jdg 4:17). Sisera does not suspect any danger from Heber's wife, Jael.[32] She appears gentle and responds with generosity to his request for help (Jdg 4:18-19). So the Antichrist will not suspect the humble of

---

[32] The Kenites were descendants of Jethro the Midianite, father-in-law of Moses. Not true sons of Abraham, Heber's household had separated themselves from their brothers who remained in Judah and moved north to Galilee. That these, in the person of Jael, turn on and destroy Sisera, can be read as a hidden hint that the last generation of Jews will become those holy Saints who overcome the antichrist.

God will defeat him. At the head of this section are the verses which relate what happened next (Jdg 4:21-22). Deborah retells the events with the eternal rejoicing:

Jael... put her left hand to the nail, and her right hand to the workman's mallet. And she struck Sisera, seeking in his head a place for the wound, and strongly piercing his temples. Between her feet, he was ruined. He fainted away and passed on. He curled up before her feet, and he lay there lifeless and miserable. (Jdg 5:26-27)

So Sisera met his miserable end.[33] The enemy of God's People lay down in exhausted sleep, hidden under Jael's cloak, and he never woke up. He died in his sleep, his brains exploding. The dramatic scene, told simply in Hebrew, is always evocative: *"he passed from the numbness of sleep into the numbness of death"* (Jdg 4:21 Knox). This is the *"second death"* (Apoc 21:8), the spiritual death of the damned which follows their biological death: *"And so, joining deep sleep to death, he fell unconscious and died"* (Jdg 4:21). Moments before dying, Sisera had said to Jael: *"if anyone arrives, questioning you and saying, 'Could there be any man here?' you shall respond, 'There is no one'"* (Jdg 4:20). So he identified himself as *"no one"* (אין), as if he had never been.[34] So futile is the work of evil.

---

[33] The sorrow of Sisera's mother is heart-breaking (Jdg 5:28-30).

[34] This word is used before the creation of man when: *"there was no man to work the land"* (Gen 2:5). St Irenæus, *Adversus Haereses*, V, 30, 4, links the futility of Antichrist's existence with *"The beast that you saw, was, and is not, and is soon to ascend from the abyss... the beast who was and is not"* (Apoc 17:8).

Jael achieved victory for the good by approaching Sisera *"softly"* (לָאט), "secretly", as if connected with mysteries, the supernatural. These mysteries can have a positive interpretation, such as for Ruth approaching Boaz *"softly"* (Rth 3:7), prefiguring Mary being beside Jesus on Calvary. Or they can have a negative connotation, as with the enchantments of Pharaoh's wizards trying to imitate or fake God's miracles (Ex 7:22; 8:7,18; Is 19:3).

Thanks to supernatural help, and signifying God's true power, the blow inflicted by Jael was mighty as the Apocalypse: she "blasted" (תָּקַע) the peg into the Antichrist's head, just as God raised a sudden and powerful wind, or Spirit, to "blast" the locust plague out of Egypt (Ex 10:19). תָּקַע is the "blast" of trumpets to gather all Israel at the tent when they are to be rescued from their enemies — as for Armageddon (Num 10:3-9).[35] Hence it is used for Joshua bringing down Jericho's walls (Josh 6:1-21). Similarly, it is used for the "thrust" of Ehud's dagger into the antichrist Eglon King of Moab, killing him (Jdg 3:21), as also for the trumpet "blast" by which Ehud then gathered all Israel for the decisive battle against the Moabites which won Israel a long period of peace (eighty years' peace; Jael won forty: Jdg 3:27,30; 5:32, a hint of the peaceful reign of Mary's Immaculate Heart). Echoing all this, it describes Gideon's decisive use of the trumpet (Jdg 6:34; 7:18-22) and, playing later in the same concert, as sounded by Joab, Solomon, Jeremiah and Ezekiel. Isaiah's *"blast of the trumpet"* prophecies God gathering the

---

[35] Fifty of seventy times that תָּקַע is used in the OT concern the *"blast"* of trumpets.

nations after the Crucifixion.[36] Appreciating all this, it is coherent to conclude that just as Sisera's temple was crushed, "blasted", so will be the Temple of the Antichrist.[37]

Who then was Jael? Her remaining in her tent while the battle raged does not indicate a timid passivity. As homemaker Jael is fully feminine, free from the insecurities of our own age whereby confused women seek to become men. Jael is contemplative, watchful, undistracted and ready for the opportunity to act decisively. She *"went out"* both to satan's chief, Sisera, and to God's chief, Barak, and both followed her instructions.[38] So Mary rules. Thanks to her alertness, clear thinking, kindness (with milk and butter) and courage, Jael defeated Israel's key enemy, and so were sung words which put us in mind of Mary: *"Blessed among women is Jael, the wife of Heber the Kenite. And blessed is she in her tabernacle"* (Jdg 5:24; cf. Lk 1:42).[39] Similar words were said

---

[36] *"All inhabitants of the world, you who dwell upon the earth: when the sign will have been elevated on the mountains, you will see, and you will hear the blast of the trumpet"* (Is 18:4) — the sign elevated on the mountains is the Cross.

[37] יָקַע is also used for more tragic cases: the fixing of Saul's dead body to the walls of Bethshan (1 Sam 31:10) and his head to the temple of Dagon (1 Chron 10:10); and the killing of the rebel Absalom, another figure of the Antichrist (2 Sam 18:14).

[38] *"Therefore, Jael went out to meet Sisera, and she said to him: 'Enter to me, my lord. Enter, you should not be afraid.' And he entered her tent, and having been covered by her with a cloak…"* (Jdg 4:18). *"And behold, Barak arrived, in pursuit of Sisera. And Jael, going out to meet him, said to him, 'Come, and I will show you the man whom you are seeking.' And when he had entered her tent, he saw Sisera lying dead, with the spike fixed in his temples"* (Jdg 4:21).

[39] Subsequently, on Calvary, Mary did not waver. But the Apostles had faltered, as was long ago prefigured in Barak's hesitation to fight. *"I [Deborah] will go indeed with thee [Barak], but at this time the victory shall not be attributed to thee, because Sisara shall be delivered into the hand of a woman"* (Jdg 4:9 DRB).

of Mary following her perfect *Fiat*, a moment encapsulating all Jael's virtues, and entailing also satan's defeat. Jael's meaning in life and her joy in Heaven is to point to Our Lady.

Does Our Lady defeat satan at the Annunciation, or on Calvary, or at her Dormition, or in the lives of the saints, or at the Apocalypse? All of these. The first three are one, united in the simplicity of Mary's will. For the last two we may think of Our Lady reigning in Heaven and there moving the hearts of the faithful on earth who are devoted to her, who will be the foot soldiers carrying out her victory. Thus besides Jael driving the tabernacle peg into Sisera's head, as Mary on earth, we also have Deborah commanding the army and singing from the mountain heights, as Mary in Heaven.[40] Barak's ten thousand who went to battle on Deborah's order are the souls devoted to Mary.

In the end their victory is total. Deborah represents heavenly Mary, who, by her maternal care, successfully raises souls for God, which is our final end. Beforehand, we read: *"the paths rested"* (Jdg 5:6 DRB), which means "the ways to the sanctuary of God were unfrequented" (according to Bishop Challoner's commentary). We might think of recent lockdowns and *Traditionis custodes*. Therefore God's People were left weak, without heroes: *"the strong men ceased, and they rested in Israel, until Deborah rose up, until a mother*

---

[40] Deborah *"was sitting under a palm tree, which was called by her name, between Ramah and Bethel, on Mount Ephraim. And the sons of Israel went up to her for every judgment"* (Jdg 4:5). The tree with her name on it signifies the Cross. The heights of Mount Ephraim are, on the map, directly above Bethlehem and Jerusalem, suggesting a progress, an ascending, from there.

rose up in Israel" (Jdg 5:7). As Deborah strengthened Israel's army, so Mary strengthens the Church Militant. This, Mary did for the Apostles from the Passion through Pentecost to her Dormition, and the same she achieves from Heaven whenever the Church hierarchy has recourse to her, for *"the sons of Israel went up to her for every judgment"* (Jdg 4:5).

A precursor of the Blessed Mother, Deborah has her Magnificat, too:

> *Rise up, rise up, O Deborah! Rise up, rise up, and speak a canticle!... The remnants of the people were saved. The Lord contended with the strong.* (Jdg 5:12)

Mary is our Mother who has risen up to Heaven. Her canticle is so important that the Church sings it every day at Vespers, assuring us of what our eyes might not see: that we have nothing to fear from the strong of this world, no matter the apparent odds. God's arm is strong, He will rescue His People in accordance with His ancient promises.

> *He hath shewed might in his arm: he hath scattered the proud in the conceit of their heart. He hath put down the mighty from their seat, and hath exalted the humble.* (Lk 1:51-52 DRB)

Mary understood all this from reading the OT. And it pleases God to demonstrate the truth of it all in her. The next story, in its own way, expresses the same truth, and again with vivid drama that makes it unforgettable.

ONE WOMAN: CITADEL OF BRIGHTNESS

Then Abimelech, setting out from there, arrived at the town of Thebez, which he surrounded and besieged with his army. Now there was, in the midst of the city, a high tower, to which men and women were fleeing together, with all the leaders of the city. And, having very strongly sealed the gate, they were standing on the roof of the tower to defend themselves. And Abimelech, drawing near the tower, fought valiantly. And approaching the gate, he strove to set it on fire. And behold, one woman, throwing a fragment of a millstone from above, struck the head of Abimelech, and broke his skull. And he quickly called to his armour bearer, and said to him, 'Draw your sword and strike me, otherwise it may be said that I was slain by a woman.' And, doing as he was ordered, he killed him. And when he was dead, all those of Israel who were with him returned to their homes. And so did God repay the evil that Abimelech had done against his father by killing his seventy brothers.

— Jdg 9:50-56

In his life and in his death Abimelech prefigures the Antichrist. To gain total political control he asked the men of Shechem:

Which is better for you: that seventy men, all the sons of Jerubbaal, should rule over you, or that one man should rule over you? (Jdg 9:2)

They gave Abimelech *"seventy pieces of silver"* from the temple of an idol (Jdg 9:4), which money he used to hire soulless assassins to murder his seventy brothers.[41] The combination of idolatry, money, murder and seizing total power represents the Antichrist working with financiers to usurp the sovereignty of all the nations of the world (signified by the number seventy), cruelly robbing countries of their freedom.[42]

But the youngest brother, Jotham, escaped. His name means "Yahweh is Perfect". He represents Jesus Christ in that he ascended a mountain and spoke a parable against the men of Shechem, announcing a blessing or a curse depending upon the intention and purity of their hearts in choosing Abimelech as king to reign over them (Jdg 9:7-20). It was by the same Mount Gerazim, with Mount Ebal, that Joshua spoke for God

---

[41] *"He went to his father's house… and he killed his brothers, the sons of Jerubbaal, seventy men, upon one stone. And there remained only Jotham, the youngest son of Jerubbaal, and he was in hiding"* (Jdg 9:5); *"one stone"* for human sacrifices suggests a demonic altar. Meanwhile, Jotham being *"in hiding"* speaks of Jesus' mysterious ways: being taken by Jospeh with Mary before the slaughter of the Innocents to "hide" in Egypt; His hidden life in Nazareth until the public ministry; taking refuge outside Israel during His ministry; and even His Divinity hidden in the tent of His Flesh, as also today in the Holy Eucharist.

[42] Symbolising all the nations of the world with the number seventy derives from Gen 10, where seventy nations are listed as descending from the three sons of Noah. St Luke's Gospel alludes to this number, but while some ancient manuscripts have seventy, others have seventy-two (Lk 10:1,17). We could say there are seventy natural nations plus two supernatural: satan's City of Man and Christ's City of God. As Gideon had seventy sons by his wives and then fathered Abimelech by a concubine (Jdg 8:30-31), we may understand the seventy to represent all the nations of the world; Abimelech as the 'nation' of evil; and Jotham as Christendom.

to all Israel, to set out blessings or curses for them to choose (Dt 11:29; 27:12; Josh 8:33).

As Joshua's words were proven true, so Jotham's judgement was fulfilled to the letter (Jdg 9:56-57). A house divided like satan's cannot stand. *"The Lord put a very grievous spirit between Abimelech and the inhabitants of Shechem, who began to detest him..."* (Jdg 9:23). They plotted his overthrow. Hearing of this *"Abimelech rose up, with all his army, by night"* (Jdg 9:34) — night, when evil operates, hidden from the sight of men — and using treachery and deceit and ruthless violence he *"took the city, and killed the people that were in it; and he razed the city and sowed it with salt"* (Jdg 9:45). The last survivors of the city's population sought refuge in the citadel, the Tower of Shechem. Abimelech and his men approached, each laying wood at the foot of the tower, then setting it all on fire so that *"by smoke and fire, one thousand persons died, men and women together, the occupants of the tower of Shechem"* (Jdg 9:49). But Abimelech also would reap what he sowed. His success was about to come to a crashing end.

Shechem represented the City of Man, and its tower the strongest thereof, yet all were defeated. Meanwhile another city, Thebez, represents the City of God, and those who took refuge in its tower represent the remnant with unconquerable devotion to Jesus through Mary. Abimelech tried exactly the same method against Thebez as he had against Shechem, planning to burn it. Thebez means brightness, but it would be a brightness other than fire which shone from here.

There was a woman, made anonymous by Scripture to signify her humility, whom we may call the "woman of Thebez", woman of brightness, of shining splendour, ultimately even *"a woman clothed with the sun, and the moon was under her feet"* (Apoc 12:1). It was her enemy Abimelech under her feet, at the foot of the tower. Initially he took most of the city, as most of the Church will go down in apostasy and persecution. But those who keep close to the Woman, who have recourse to her protection, survive the diabolical inferno which engulfs others.[43]

As noted, there was, *"in the midst of the city, a high tower"*, a strong tower, and all the men and women and leaders of the city fled there, taking refuge, and went up to the roof for defence, the gate being *"sealed"*, סָגַר. The same word describes Adam's side being *"closed"* after the rib was removed (Gen 2:21); and Noah's ark being *"sealed"* once all flesh entered into her (Gen 7:16); as Lot *"blocked"* the door so the Sodomites could not assault the angels (Gen 19:6,10). All these associations may put us in mind of the Church, who is meant to keep the evil outside; keep the good inside; and who receives life from the wound of her Lord. Significantly, in the heavenly city the gates are not shut, for there is no more night, no enemy who can attack (Apoc 21:25).

Entering the tower, a stronghold, represents taking refuge in Mary. They are safest who ascend to spiritual heights, out of reach of the world, close to the *"woman"*, secure under her

---

[43] By the ancient prayer *Sub tuum præsidium* we fly to the protection of the Mother of God to "deliver us always from all dangers".

protection while being active in defence (Jdg 9:51). That a tower stands for Our Lady is supported by a Marian interpretation of the Canticle of Canticles, from which the Litany of Loreto honours Mary as *Turris Davidica, Turris eburnea* ("Tower of David, Tower of ivory..."). The first appellation has connotations of strength and defence with ramparts and shields, the second of a city's ornamentation and beauty.[44] Mary excels in both. In fact Our Lady is the opposite of the Tower of Babel. Mary reaches from earth to Heaven and is made by God to unify all peoples in Him.

"Abimelech, drawing near the tower, fought vigorously. And approaching the gate (θύρα), he strove to set it on fire" (Jdg 9:52), like the devil trying to ignite sin. He failed, for the *"gate"*, or *"door"*, is Christ, Who said: *"I am the door (θύρα)"* (Jn 10:9). Also indicating Jesus, in Hebrew פֶּתַח refers to the *"door"* or *"entrance"* to the tabernacle (Ex 26:36); likewise to the Temple; to the King's House; to the Holy City; and the *"door"* of the tent where Abraham encountered the Trinity (Gen 18:1-2). פֶּתַח is also the entrance to Noah's ark (Gen 6:16); and where the blood of the lamb protects from the angel of death (Ex 12:22). Because there is no sin in Christ, sin lies outside the *"door"*, waiting in ambush, but unable to

---

[44] *"Your neck is like the tower of David, which was built with ramparts: a thousand shields are hanging from it, all the armour of the strong"* (Cant 4:4). *"Your neck is like a tower of ivory. Your eyes like the fish ponds at Heshbon, which are at the entrance to the daughter of the multitude. Your nose is like the tower of Lebanon, which looks out toward Damascus"* (Cant 7:4). For strength and beauty together, see: *"The men of Arvad and your army were upon your walls round about, and men of Gamad were in your towers; they hung their shields upon your walls round about; they made perfect your beauty"* (Ezek 27:11 RSVCE).

enter through Him (Gen 4:7). The aggressive rapists of Sodom could not find the *"door"* to enter in (Gen 19:11).

Neither could Abimelech enter through the door. Frustrated in his approach, what was it exactly that crushed his head? The word רֶכֶב appears 120 times in the OT. Only three times does it denote an *"upper millstone"* (Jdg 9:53), as thrown down by the woman of Thebez. Otherwise, over 95 per cent of its uses refer to chariots or their riders, including the chariot on which Elijah was translated up to heaven (2 Kngs 2:11). Here then we may think of a chariot descending from heaven to crush the Antichrist's head, sent down by the woman, the Blessed Virgin Mary, the very vessel in whom the Sacred Humanity of Our Lord rode into the world.[45] Variously Mary is represented by the holy city, and by the central tower, and by the woman at the top of the tower, and by the upper millstone she threw down onto Abimelech.

The events in Thebez also illustrate the self-destruction of evil. The *"millstone from above struck the head of Abimelech, and broke his skull"*, but it did not quite finish him off. Instead:

> *he quickly called to his armour bearer, and said to him, 'Draw your sword and strike me, otherwise it may be said that I was slain by a woman.' And, doing as he was ordered, he killed him.* (Jdg 9:54)

---

[45] St Catherine of Siena honours Our Lady as "the intermediary, the real chariot of fire, who in conceiving within herself the Word, God's only-begotten Son, brought and gave us the fire of love — for He is love Himself."

Truly evil destroys itself by its own mouth, its own commands, its own collaborators — a theme we will encounter repeatedly. It is not, after all, an easy matter to heave a millstone from a parapet, certainly not a light thing to aim with precision. Rather than say the woman was lucky, we may say her initiative was correct, her timing was perfect, and Providence was with her to guide the stone down. We discern a combination of factors at work: the action of the woman, who is Mary; the tendency of evil to self-destruction, which is inevitable; and the Providence of God, which brings everything to His Purpose.

The word רָצַץ for *"crushing"* Abimelech's head is that used when praising God Who *"shattered the heads of the serpents in the waters; You have broken* (רִצַּצְתָּ) *the heads of Leviathan"* (Ps 73:13-14), the sea dragon, satan. The content of the Psalm suits the end times: God's people ask if they will be cast off unto the end, for the enemy has seized the sanctuary, devastated it, seeking to end the worship of God and, in unbearable arrogance, raised himself to be glorified in God's Holy Place. So it will be at the end.

Are we close to this end? The seizure of the sanctuaries lamented in Psalm 73, which the Church prays every Thursday at Sext, resonates with the sense of abandonment suffered by simple Catholics:[46]

---

[46] Before evil is finally crushed, we may feel as if the Church herself is being crushed. The Israelites, choosing to serve idols, *"abandoned the Lord, and they did not worship him"* (Jdg 10:6). Consequently they were *"crushed"* by the Philistines and Ammonites (Jdg 10:8), precisely as God warned would result from infidelity (Dt 28:33). The end times, too, will be marked by infidelity, by the great apostasy.

Lift up thy hands against their pride... see what things the enemy hath done wickedly in the sanctuary... They have set up their ensigns... the pride of them that hate thee ascendeth continually. (Ps 73:3,23)

This is the distressing truth today. Infiltrators have wreckovated the sanctuaries of Catholic churches. Unfaithful priests have polluted her holy places with rainbow flags — ensigns of pure pride. Perfidious prelates have introduced idols to be honoured in the Vatican, Pachamama being preferred to the Blessed Virgin Mary. The impious hierarchy who tread upon the hearts of the faithful this way should hear Amos telling the Israelites they will be taken away with fishhooks for *"crushing"* the poor (Amos 4:1-2).

God commands the reverse, that we have charity upon the *"crushed"* and free him (Is 58:6). Jesus covers this in saying:

Therefore, all things whatsoever that you wish that men would do to you, do so also to them. For this is the law and the prophets. (Mt 7:12)

For those who spurn the law and prophets unto the end, for those who refuse to discover charity, the episode in Thebez ends, as will the world, with retribution for the unrepentant:

And so did God repay the evil that Abimelech had done against his father by killing his seventy brothers. The Shechemites also were given retribution for what they had done, and the curse of Jotham, the son of Jerubbaal, fell upon them. (Jdg 9:56-57)

Once Abimelech, precursor of the Antichrist, was dead, *"all those of Israel who were with him returned to their homes"* (Jdg 9:55). The last word here is מָקוֹם, the famous Hebrew term for the "place" chosen from eternity for the Temple. Thus when each minor antichrist is defeated, men return again to the True Temple, Jesus Christ. When the last Antichrist is done, satan's head crushed, those who are not with him will return to God, to the ultimate home of Heaven. Here we may meet Mary face to face. Also Jael. And the woman of Thebez. And, causing hearts to blaze with joy, one to whom we now turn: the daughter of Jephthah.

JEPHTHAH'S DAUGHTER: η θυγατηρ μονογενης αυτω αγαπητη

> *When Jephthah returned to Mizpah, to his own house,*
> *his only daughter met him with timbrels and dances. For*
> *he had no other children. And upon seeing her, he tore*
> *his garments, and he said: 'Alas, my daughter! You have*
> *cheated me, and you yourself have been cheated. For I*
> *opened my mouth to the Lord, and I can do nothing*
> *else.' And she answered him, 'My father, if you have*
> *opened your mouth to the Lord, do to me whatever you*
> *have promised, since victory has been granted to you, as*
> *well as vengeance against your enemies.'*

— Jdg 11:34-36

Jephthah, a mighty warrior, was a saviour of Israel, delivering God's people from their enemies. Thereby he prefigures the Messiah. Notably, Jephthah was rejected by his own half-brothers on grounds which carry a Marian note, that he was born *"of another woman"* (Jdg 11:2). Although they meant this disparagingly, we may think of the uniqueness of Our Lady, who is an other woman. Hence, *"the Spirit of the Lord rested upon Jephthah"* (Jdg 11:29), a phrase and a reality pointing ahead to Jesus (Mt 3:16; Jn 1:32).[47]

---

[47] We might think too of the exceptional blessings granted to God's *"servant"* Caleb, because he was *"full of another spirit"* (Num 14:24). Caleb did not suffer the spirit of fear which dominated ten of his fellow spies sent by Moses into the Holy Land. But with Joshua, *"a man in whom is the Spirit"* (Num 27:18 DRB), Caleb gained a portion in Israel (Jos 14:30).

Like Jephthah's half-brothers, the Ephraimites also refused to support him in defending Israel (Jdg 12:2). Unfazed:

avoiding them, he lived in the land of Tob. And men who were indigent and robbers joined with him, and they followed him as their leader. (Jdg 11:3)

This reminds us of David when he was on the run:

and all those left in distress, or oppressed by debt to strangers, or bitter in soul, gathered themselves to him. And he became their leader. (1 Sam 22:2)

Both Jephthah and David prefigure Jesus, given *"His own did not accept Him"* (Jn 1:11). Hence He gathered fishermen and tax collectors and zealots, and became their master, and with these He conquered the world. Jesus does not turn away the lowly or sinners who seek Him.

Next comes an ominous line, followed by the most tragic shock in the OT. Jephthah vowed to the Lord that if he were granted victory in battle over the Ammonites, then whatever *"will be the first to come forth from the doors of my house to meet me... the same will I offer as a holocaust to the Lord"* (Jdg 11:31). The Lord indeed delivered the enemy into his hands, so a holocaust was owed. Perhaps Jephthah was expecting an alert goat to exit his house first, a prized ram or favourite lamb. Such animals could dwell in the house of their owner (2 Sam 12:3). But Jephthah does not seem the tender type to have pets, and a single animal does not seem like an appropriate price for a victory in war. On the other hand, what kind of a brute was he if he were expecting a devoted slave to appear first to greet him? In any case, what actually happened has been distressing to read ever since:

> *Jephthah came to his home at Mizpah; and behold, his daughter came out to meet him with timbrels and with dances; she was his only child; beside her he had neither son nor daughter. And when he saw her, he rent his clothes, and said, 'Alas, my daughter! you have brought me very low, and you have become the cause of great trouble to me; for I have opened my mouth to the Lord, and I cannot take back my vow.'* (Jdg 11:34-35 RSVCE)[48]

She was his daughter, his only-begotten, his beloved, and apart from her he had no sons or daughters. With such a description, we cannot but think of Isaac, except his life was spared, unlike hers.[49] The *"timbrels... with dances"* remind us of Miriam, sister of Aaron, who had come with timbrels, dancing and singing when God had hurled the Egyptian army into the sea (Ex 15:20).[50] Now here was Jephthah's virgin daughter, also rejoicing over the defeat of the enemy. She would pay the heaviest price for it, for it fell to her to be the first to come forth from her father's house. She stuns us with her submissive reaction:

---

[48] The last words here are *"cannot apostasise [ἀποστρέψαι]"* (Jdg 11:35).

[49] Compare Gen 22:2 with "ἡ θυγάτηρ αὐτοῦ... καὶ αὕτη μονογενὴς αὐτῷ ἀγαπητή καὶ οὐκ ἔστιν αὐτῷ πλὴν αὐτῆς υἱὸς ἢ θυγάτηρ" (Jdg 11:34).

[50] The same instruments being used to honour the Ark of God (1 Chron 13:8) and in divine worship (Ps 149:3; Jer 31:4).

*My father, if you have opened your mouth to the Lord,
do to me whatever you have promised, since victory has
been granted to you, as well as vengeance against your
enemies.* (Jdg 11:36)

Such a spirit, yielding all for God's sake, anticipates the Virgin
Mary, whose willing sacrifice on Calvary, lovingly enduring
the seven sorrows of the *via Matris*, was even more costly
than death.

This fixity of Mary's will in union with God's we see
already in Nazareth when Mary asked the Archangel: *"How
shall this be done, since I do not know man?"* (Lk 1:34) This
question was not a prevarication from an unsure will. Rather it
was for the sake of understanding, to know she was not being
asked to violate her vow of virginity, her total self-gift to God,
for the sake of conceiving a son. So Jephthah's daughter did
not hesitate to fulfil her father's will, but requested:

*that I may wander the hillsides for two months, and that
I may mourn my virginity with my companions.* [After
this she] *returned to her father, and he did to her just as
he had vowed, though she knew no man.* (Jdg 11:37-39)

She asked for two months, not to rethink but to *"mourn her
virginity"*. This included acknowledging that her biological
family line ended with her, and still she gave herself. She saw
the happiness which married life promised, and still she gave
herself. She was made a holocaust. For this all generations
have remembered and honoured her.

*From this, the custom grew up in Israel, and the practice
has been preserved, such that, after each year passes,
the daughters of Israel convene as one, and they lament
the daughter of Jephthah, the Gileadite, for four days.*
(Jdg 11:39-40)

To this day she is remembered, although not nearly on the
same scale as the memorials and celebrations and feasts
devoted to the Mother of God. This should help us to
appreciate that though the sacrifice of Jephthah's daughter was
total, yet incomparably greater was the sacrifice of Mary. It is
heroic to give one's life; it is ineffable to give one's divine
Son. Most mothers would sooner die than see their own child
die: how much more when that Mother is Mary and that Child
is Jesus.

Despite the difference in scale, the parallels between
Jephthah's daughter and the Virgin Mary indicate that the
Mother of God's victory runs seamlessly from her *Fiat* at the
Incarnation to her sacrifice on Calvary and onward to her
eschatological triumph. For Jephthah's daughter was
immediately willing to fulfil her father's word; then, when the
time came, she gave herself unmurmuring in total sacrifice.
Ever since she has been celebrated by the daughters of Israel,
and now by the Church, on earth and above all in Heaven. Her
loss is, in reality, great gain; so also what Our Lady lost on
Calvary was returned in untold glory on Easter Sunday to the
advantage of all.

There are further parallels. All Catholics know the victory
is primarily Christ's, hence Jephthah did the fighting. Yet by

participation the victory is also Mary's, who freely offered her Son — Soul of her soul. Hence we see Jephthah's daughter gave herself entirely for her father's cause, for God's cause. The earlier events were fashioned by God to prefigure the latter. Jephthah's daughter was the first to come forth from his house to greet him, and so it fell to her to pay the price for the victory. The Virgin Mary, God's unique daughter, was the first to come forth, as it were, from God's House, the House of Israel, to greet God (not the first in time, but the first in fullness, in excellence). Receiving the Lord (as Mother, Lk 1:38) when He came, it fell to Mary to suffer more than any other creature for the sake of His victory.

Jephthah's daughter suffered her agony, hiding it under her simplicity and concern for her father. We can be sure Jephthah felt the loss of his daughter his whole life long, bitterly regretting opening his mouth with a catastrophic oath. Nobody defends his oath, albeit Church Fathers say many have been instructed by it not to make vows rashly. They maintain that vows made by the immature may be dispensed, while in Jephthah's case, it was invalidated alone by its irrationality. We cannot make a gift of folly to God. Yet God allowed the events to roll out as they did to instruct us on Mary's immolation on Calvary.

Jephthah lamented that his daughter had *"brought me very low"* (Jdg 11:35). It is the same word, כָּרַע, used for Judah crouching low like a lion (Gen 49:9) in the messianic prophecy, and later for Israel lying down lionlike in fearless invincibility (Num 24:9). In these cases the lion crouches in readiness to spring up, or sleeps to waken when it will, both symbolising the Messiah Who resurrected with a supernatural roar. Like a crouching lion, Jesus went down into death in order to rise (Mt 16:21; Jn 20:9; Rom 14:9); and like a sleeping lion, He rose when He chose (Jn 10:17-18).

This same word, כָּרַע, also occurs three times in a single verse for dead Sisera at Jael's feet (Jdg 5:27), each time in combination with נָפַל (*"fell"*), as the *"deep sleep"* which *"fell"* on Adam and Abram point to Christ's Crucifixion. By groaning that he is *"brought very low"*, Jephthah is expressing his own crucifixion at the loss of his daughter. Was Mary's deepest pain on Calvary not for her Son? Was Jesus' deepest pain on Calvary not for His Mother?[51] Similarly Jephthah suffered an unspeakable agony in losing his daughter. Counting for him as penance, his purified soul was accounted acceptable to God (1 Sam 12:11; Heb 11:32).

We are upset by this story. But would Jephthah's daughter, given the chance, rewrite this piece of history, so that the tragedy of her father's oath be removed, that she be allowed another chance at life without the trauma of untimely death? She would surely have no interest, for she has undoubtedly an honoured place in Paradise, one of the closest companions of Mary. She is perfectly content with God's arrangement and her role in it. Her life is high in Heaven.

---

[51] At La Salette and Fatima, Our Lady asked for penance on account of sins against God, including sacrileges against the Holy Eucharist. At Pontevedra, Jesus asked for acts of reparation for injuries against His Mother's Immaculate Heart.

It is worth conceding, too, that her glory is indirectly thanks to the Ammonites, the enemies. Had they not attacked, no such sacrifice would have been required. We bristle against the onslaught of evil in this life, but in the next we will praise God for all the good He has drawn out of it. If we are fully conscious of this, we need not even bristle under attack, as the angelic St Stephen asked God to forgive his persecutors even as they stoned him to death (Acts 7:54-59). He could see the reward of Heaven outweighed all suffering.

The Ammonites pressed Israel hard as mortal enemies. Jephthah offered an unknown soul to God in order that the Ammonites be defeated. After the victory was granted, he discovered who that soul was: his daughter. There was no other more dear to him. Generations later, David would win greater, more decisive victories against these enemy Ammonites (2 Sam 10:6-14; 12:26-31), losing his child in the midst of it (2 Sam 12:18). Finally came Jesus, who defeated the very worst enemy, satan. His dear Mother, spiritual daughter, gave herself for this victory and essentially suffered martyrdom for it. It is not easy for us to grasp this. But Jephthah's daughter gives us a glimpse, she who gave herself for the sake of Israel's victory, saying simply:

My father, if you have opened your mouth to the Lord, do to me whatever you have promised, since victory has been granted to you, as well as vengeance against your enemies. (Jdg 11:36)

She could have taken the opportunity of her two-month retreat in the mountains to abscond and escape her young death. But she was the price of her father's oath for his victory (Jdg 11:12-33). If the oath were not kept, so she thought, then Israel's enemies might quickly recover and threaten the very existence of the Holy Land with unspeakable consequences for salvation. Jephthah's daughter demonstrates that when the worst persecution comes, it will not be by tent pegs nor by upper millstones that the war is won, but essentially by self-sacrifice, that is, total consecration. Our fight is not against flesh and blood, but spiritual (Eph 6:12).

In this story, though both father and daughter suffer great pain, naturally our sympathy is much more with the daughter than with Jephthah. Might this be God's way to highlight Mary's suffering on Calvary, lest we otherwise notice only that of her Son? Can we say God accepted Mary's self-sacrifice with the inflexible surety that Jephthah did his daughter's? Perhaps we recoil from drawing a parallel which so elevates Jephthah to represent God. But the parallel has substance.

Firstly, in the sovereignty of God's will which, like Jephthah's, we cannot scrutinise.

Secondly, in Jephthah's confidence in his daughter's devotion to him, for he expected her free cooperation. Likewise God did of Mary.

Thirdly, if we consider Jephthah's pain. Perhaps we are reluctant to do this, for we would sooner berate him: first for making the oath, second for keeping it. But we are no better than he, for we by our sins caused the Crucifixion of Christ, making us infinitely culpable. So what is the meaning of Jephthah's pain? Little is written about it:

> he rent his clothes, and said, 'Alas, my daughter! you have brought me very low, and you have become the cause of great trouble to me'. (Jud 11:35 RSVCE)

These expressions of distress are not to be dismissed. Especially they are to be considered if Jephthah points us to the Father. We miss the point of the Father's love if looking at Calvary we simply say God is impassible so suffered no pain, concluding that the whole cost the Father nothing. It is true that God as God cannot suffer, but that does not explain His love for us. Rather the Father and Son are One (Jn 10:30), so the suffering of His Son does reveal the Father's love for us. We cannot imagine a greater suffering, therefore we cannot imagine a greater love. And neither was God the Father indifferent to Mary's pain on Calvary. Perhaps it was the most 'distressing' thing that He has ever witnessed? (I know: God the Father cannot suffer. But that does not mean He is coldly indifferent to our pain.)

This love on Calvary ended the devil's reign, and he has been flailing ever since. God wants us to understand Mary's role in this, for she shows the perfect response of creature to Creator. To help us understand, God gives us Jephthah's daughter in prefiguration. Like St Jacinta Marto dying young, she lost in the short term but won for eternity; numberless antichrists win for passing moments but will forever bear their damnation. Both premises hurt us in this life, and both conclusions should rejoice us in the next.[52]

Finally, her self-sacrifice was offered even after the battle had already been won, so we might think it pointless. But that is not how love works. Love is total. She was more heroic still than those who stay and give their lives even after the battle is clearly lost, for she gave hers when it was harder, that is, after the battle was clearly won. For it is brave to fight for victory when the battle still might be won, and braver still to sacrifice oneself when the battle is evidently lost, in an attempt to slow down the rout and give one's comrades time to escape. At least one is spared the misery of life after defeat. But to give one's life after the battle is clearly won is apparently to lose out on the benefits of victory. That is, if we are thinking only of this world. Of course eternity matters more.

The lesson for those who end up facing the Antichrist is to remain steadfast in all circumstances whatsoever, for if we are faithful even after we think we have lost, in fact we will win. If this is hard to believe, it is why God has given throughout the Scriptures so many promises of victory!

---

[52] St Thomas, *S.Th.* Suppl., Q.94 a.3. See also 2 Macc 7:34-38.

Female Genius: Saving the City of Abel

Now Sheba had passed through all the tribes of Israel into Abel and Bethmaacah. And all the elect men had gathered together to him. And so, they went and besieged him at Abel and Bethmaacah. And they surrounded the city with siege works, and the city was blockaded. Then the entire crowd who were with Joab strove to destroy the walls. And a wise woman exclaimed from the city: 'Listen, listen, and say to Joab: Draw near, and I will speak with you.' And when he had drawn near to her, she said to him, 'Are you Joab?' And he responded, 'I am.' And she spoke in this way to him, 'Listen to the words of your handmaid.' He responded, 'I am listening.' And again she spoke: 'A word was said in the old proverb, "Those who would inquire, let them inquire in Abel." And so they would reach a conclusion. Am I not the one who responds with the truth in Israel? And yet you are seeking to overthrow the city, and to overturn a mother in Israel! Why would you cast down the inheritance of the Lord?' And responding, Joab said: 'May this be far, may this be far from me! May I not cast down, and may I not demolish. The matter is not as you said. Rather, a man from mount Ephraim, Sheba, the son of Bichri, by name, has lifted up his hand against king David. Deliver him alone, and we will withdraw from the city.' And the woman said to Joab, 'Behold, his head will be thrown down to you from the wall.' Therefore, she entered to all the people, and she spoke to them wisely. And they cut off the head of Sheba, the son of Bichri, and they threw it down to Joab. And he sounded the trumpet, and they withdrew from the city, each one to his own tent. But Joab returned to Jerusalem to the king.

— 2 Sam 20:14-22

The first thing the Bible tells us about Sheba, before we hear even his proper name, is that he was called *"a worthless man"*, a pestilent fellow, a son beyond the law (υἰὸς παράνομος, 2 Sam 20:1). In Hebrew, a *"man of Belial"* (בְּלִיַּעַל), devilish, as were his Benjaminite ancestors who had raped to death the Levite's concubine, these being also described as *"sons of Belial"* (Jdg 19:22).

Sheba instigates a massive rebellion against King David, signalling it with a blast (תָּקַע) on the shofar, or the trumpet — a hint of the last days. Seditiously he announces to all Israel that they have no portion with David, no inheritance in Judah (2 Sam 20:1). His sedition is effective, as

all of Israel separated from David, and they were following Sheba, the son of Bichri. But the men of Judah clung to their king. (2 Sam 20:2)

In this Sheba prefigures the Antichrist, for he calls all the world away from their king, away from the Holy City, provoking apostasy, making the people disciples of himself (Apoc 13:4,8). Only Judah, the remnant, remains true to David, their King, the Anointed One, that is Jesus. Sheba was the son of *"Bichri"*, which means "the one born first". Here we might think of Cain, or even Lucifer, who brought into existence as prince of all the angels. Being first among creatures, Lucifer sought to claim the rights of God's true Firstborn, the Son of God, Who is generated from all eternity. In hopeless imitation of the devil, Sheba wants to usurp the throne of God's chosen king, David. Thus Sheba was a son of Lucifer, a spawn of satan.

Sheba's insurrection takes place shortly after another one by Absalom. David senses that this time round it will be much more dangerous than before (2 Sam 20:6), just as the final Antichrist will be more evil than his forerunners.[53] Although David fled when Absalom revolted, for he had compassion for his son, even if misplaced, this time he opts for war. Being old, David sends his officer Amasa to lead the army against Sheba. Soon after, he sends reinforcements, among them the accomplished warrior Joab.

The king's strength of purpose after his bout of weakness in the face of his son Absalom's insurrection may cause us to think of popes who failed to find the phenomenal strength required to discipline their dissenting and heretical bishops, causing great grief amid the flock (2 Sam 19:4-8). But by this very process the whole Body learns to be strong for the final confrontation, as David rediscovers, being decisive when the time comes to deal with Sheba's insurrection.

---

[53] Absalom (meaning 'father of peace') revolted against the natural order and against God's order, that is against his own father, the anointed king, and against the proper priesthood. This is all bad enough, but Sheba was worse, his appellations indicating attachment to the devil.

Still, not everything goes smoothly. David's chief officers, divided by Joab's jealousy, quarrel on the way to battle. Joab mortally wounds Amasa, causing confusion and delay among their own soldiers until Amasa's bloody corpse is hidden beside the way (2 Sam 20:9-13). Doubtless there will be rivalries in the Church right until Armageddon begins.

The city where Sheba took his last stand, Abel-Bethmaacah, lies in the northern extremity of Israel, a direction associated with the evil of the Antichrist,[54] lying between Nimrod, Dan and Tyre, all three also linked with the Antichrist.[55] Here in Abel, Bichri perished — his demise counting poetically as a delayed victory for Abel, who was slain by the first antichrist, his brother Cain.[56]

Determined to defeat Sheba, Joab besieges the city, seeing the only option to be total destruction. But just as Barak for his hesitation ceded the triumph over Sisera to Jael, so here

---

[54] The association of the north with the source of evil is made by major prophets. Jeremiah said: *"From the north, an evil will spread over all the inhabitants of the earth"* (Jer 1:14). And Isaiah: *"How is it that you have fallen from heaven, O Lucifer... you said in your heart: '...I will be enthroned... on the northern parts'"* (Is 14:12-13). So in Holy Mass the deacon sings the Gospel toward the (liturgical) north, to conquer for Christ the unenlightened darkness. Likewise the subdeacon holds the text of the Last Gospel so that the celebrant can face north to read it, or in a Low Mass, the celebrant positions himself at a suitable angle, as he does for reading the Gospel of the Mass, to illustrate the same point.

[55] The root of Nimrod's name is מָרַד , meaning "rebellion". Midrashim say he hunted men to eat, sought God's place for himself, instigated the Tower of Babel, was the chief enemy of Abraham, all thoroughly evil. That the tribe of Dan will produce the Antichrist is the interpretation by some Church Fathers of Jer 8:16, and is supported by the observation that Dan is not mentioned among the twelve tribes in Heaven (Apoc 7:4-8). For Tyre's link with the Antichrist, see Ezek 28:11-19.

[56] Albeit the name of Abel the man (הֶבֶל , Hebel) is spelt differently in Hebrew to Abel the city (אָבֵל , Abel).

Joab, for acting unworthily on the way, will likewise cede the honours of victory to a woman, again one who prefigures the Blessed Virgin Mary. The woman is *"wise"* and calls herself a *"handmaid"* (2 Sam 20:16-17). She draws the commander of the king's army, Joab, close to her, and instructs him with ancient advice, a proverb: let them come to Abel for answers. She asks: *"Am I not the one who responds with the truth in Israel?"* (2 Sam 20:19). Not in murderous fury would this problem be solved, not at the cost of the whole city when it was needful only to crush the head of the rebellion. The wise woman warns Joab not to *"overturn a mother in Israel"* nor *"cast down the inheritance of the Lord"* (2 Sam 20:19), which means avoiding the slaughter of all the souls who could be saved if a Mother may apply her wisdom, thereby avoiding that the inheritance of the Lord be lost, which means not endangering potential saints for Heaven. We may think of the urgent necessity of the hierarchy heeding Fatima.

A midrash identifies this ancient woman as Sarah the daughter of Asher, one of the seventy souls *"of the house of Jacob, who went into Egypt"* (Gen 46:17,27). As a survivor of the seventy, the implication is that all the nations of the world are gathered in the city. If Joab, sometimes too quick with his weapon, hurls his army at them in bloodlust, without first seeking a more prudent way, then he risks doing the Antichrist's work for him.

Avoiding this error, the woman promises a simple and speedy victory. She goes *"to all the people, and she spoke to them wisely"* (2 Sam 2:22). Thus Mary convinces us of the still more excellent way, and the people are persuaded, thereby saving their own souls. Heeding the call of their mother, they regret their rebellion, and *"they cut off the head of Sheba, the son of Bichri"* (2 Sam 2:22) and throw it down over the wall to Joab who surely sees therein: *"Wisdom is better than weapons of war"* (Eccl 9:18). For Catholics who heed their Mother, this means a firm rejection of personal and social sin, so the devil has no part in or among us.

Whether the devil has no part in us or whether indeed he has a grip on our soul, we rely on our heavenly Mother. The earlier antichrist Abimelech had been fighting to get into the city, but the woman of Thebez saved the inhabitants by throwing a millstone down on his head. It was more desperate this time, as the antichrist Sheba had already infiltrated the city, but it availed him nothing. There was within a woman's voice which guided the people to act with wisdom. They received her word, and they overcame the enemy in their midst, winning peace for all, in the city and in the kingdom.

Some eight centuries later, a still more grievous situation pertained under the madman Antiochus IV Epiphanes (175-164 BC). It is well worth our taking a diversion here to look into this, remembering the wise woman's wistful warning against overturning *"a mother in Israel"*. Whoever tries to do this, even though he thinks he succeeds, will in fact lose big.

Usurping political control in Judea, Antiochus forbade circumcision and the keeping of the Sabbath, contaminated the Temple in Jerusalem with prostitution and Greek idols, and executed countless Jews. He is the OT's clearest prefiguration of the Antichrist. Again, it was a mother, together with her seven sons, who put him utterly to shame.

The family was apprehended and scourged, and ordered to blaspheme, but the firstborn responded: *"We are ready to die, rather than to betray the laws that our fathers received from God"* (2 Macc 7:2). Heroically he endured diabolical tortures, giving an example to his brothers until they,

> *united with the mother, exhorted one another to die with fortitude, saying: 'The Lord God will perceive the truth, and he will be consoled in us, in the way that Moses declared in the profession of the canticle: "And in his servants, he will be consoled".'* (2 Macc 7:4-6)

This is profound, to think that man by his fidelity can console God![57] One by one, the following generations of brothers were threatened, tortured and killed, yet all gave unfading witness to the true God. All through the centuries the Church has borne martyrs and saints, inspired by the example of the Firstborn, Jesus, and comforted by the exhortations of their

---

[57] Sources and translations vary on whether *"God will be comforted"* in His servants or *"God will comfort"* His servants. *Consolor* is a deponent verb, used in the passive voice but understood in the active voice. In some cases the apparent ambiguity is beautiful. The Common of Martyrs, Pascal Time, Matins, *Responsorium* V has: *"In servis suis, alleluja, Consolabitur Deus, alleluja."* This may be understood as saying "God will comfort His servants", but it is also fitting that on the feast of the martyrs, and the reading above of 2 Macc 7:6, we can say, "God is consoled by His servants". Our willingness to suffer for Him, even suffer death, is a consolation for God Who gave His Son and Who suffered death for us. It shows we know the value of His Gift, and the prize of His company. The double *Consolamini* of Christmas Day (Matins, *Lectio* II) is certainly understood in the passive sense: *"Be comforted, be comforted, my people, saith your God"* (Is 40:1).

Mother, Mary, who is always active in the Church. So it will be for all generations of her children to the end.

An alternative reading would be to count the six elder brothers as representing the prophets before the time of Christ. After these have been tortured and executed by Antiochus, there is a mysterious hint of the Incarnation (2 Macc 7:22-23); then we come to the youngest brother, representing Jesus. Antiochus tried to sway him with promises of wealth, protection and honours (2 Macc 7:24). It parallels the devil trying to tempt Jesus with bread from stones, angelic protection and world domination (Mt 4:1-11). When this failed to move the boy, Antiochus attempted to get to him through his mother. He imagined she would not be strong enough to bear the loss of her only (remaining) son. He sought to use her to undermine his morale. The opposite happened. The *"language of the fathers"* in what follows stands for the Faith:

And so, when he had exhorted her with many words, she promised that she would counsel her son. Then, leaning towards him and mocking the cruel tyrant, she said in the language of the fathers: 'My son, take pity on me, for I carried you for nine months in my womb, and I gave you milk for three years, and I nourished you and led you through to this stage of life. I ask you, child, gaze upon heaven and earth... So shall it be that you will not fear this executioner, but... you shall accept death, so that, by this mercy, I shall receive you again with your brothers.' (2 Macc 7:25-29)

The fortitude of this Maccabean mother is recorded so that we might wonder at the fortitude of Mary. The devil sought weakness in her but found none. And the son gives us an image of Christ for our imitation:

'I, like my brothers, deliver up my soul and my body for the sake of the laws of the fathers, calling upon God so as to bring forgiveness upon our nation sooner...' Then the king [Antiochus], burning with anger, raged against this one with cruelty beyond all the rest, bearing it indignantly that he himself was derided. And so this one also died in purity, trusting in the Lord through all things. Then, last of all, after the sons, the mother also was consumed. (2 Macc 7:37-41)

Son and mother made their sacrifice. Two centuries later, Jesus' Sacred Heart was pierced with a soldier's spear, Mary's Immaculate Heart pierced by a spiritual sword.[58] They gave God all, therefore they won.

The demise of the devil, and the sure failure of the Antichrist, is foreshadowed in the miserable end of Antiochus, which was more grim than the beheaded son of Bichri:

So then, worms swarmed from his impious body, and, as he lived on in pain, his flesh fell away, and then his odorous stench oppressed the army. And him who, a little before, thought that he could touch the stars of

---

[58] St Basil of Seleucia: "As the sun surpasses all the stars in lustre, so the sorrows of Mary surpasses all the tortures of the martyrs. Therefore, the Church calls Mary the Queen of Martyrs, because her martyrdom surpassed that of all others."

heaven, no one could endure to carry, because of the intolerable stench... And, when he could not even bear his own stench, he spoke in this way: 'It is just to be subject to God, and a mortal should not consider himself equal to God.' (2 Macc 9:9-12)

The Antichrist will see his error and failure shortly before he descends to hell (cf. Dan 4:19-22). As for us, whether sin threatens us from without like Abimelech outside the tower, or has a presence in our soul as Bichri inside the city of Abel, or seems to have taken over our lives entirely as Antiochus tyrannised Judea, we have yet a mother willing to do all for our salvation. In every moment we may be strengthened by one braver than the Maccabean mother, guided by one wiser than the woman of Abel, protected by one mightier than the woman of Thebez. A mother loves her children even when they have dirtied themselves, gently cleaning them until they develop sufficient maturity to desire to keep themselves clean. Biologically, this takes perhaps two or three years. Spiritually, it may take a lifetime. For the Church as a whole, it will take until the end of time.

Finally, Joab *"sounded the trumpet"*, signalling the Last Day, *"and they withdrew from the city"*, that is, they left the city of this world, *"each one to his own tent"*, to the dwelling place prepared for them by Jesus, to each a mansion in Heaven (2 Sam 2:22; Jn 14:2).

JUDITH: BLESSED ABOVE ALL WOMEN ON EARTH

Holofernes, being very inebriated, was fast asleep, reclining on his bed. And Judith told her handmaid to stand outside before the chamber, and to watch. And Judith stood in front of the bed, praying with tears, and her lips moved in silence, saying: 'Confirm me, O Lord God of Israel, and in this hour look kindly upon the works of my hands, so that, just as you promised, you may raise up Jerusalem, your city, and so that, believing through you that this plan is able to be accomplished, I may succeed.' And when she had said this, she approached the pillar, which was at the head of the bed, and she released his blade, which was hanging tied to it. And when she had unsheathed it, she grabbed him by the hair of his head, and she said, 'Confirm me, O Lord God, in this hour.' And she struck him twice on his neck, and she cut off his head, and she took off his canopy from the pillars, and she rolled away the trunk of his body. And after a little while, she went out [and] came to the gate of the city. And Judith, from a distance, spoke to the watchmen on the walls, 'Open the gates, for God is with us, and he has acted with his power in Israel.'

— Jud 13:4-13 [59]

---

[59] The Book of Judith seems to have been written originally in Hebrew, although no such early text is extant. The SB, used here where not otherwise attributed, is a translation from the Vulgate, as is the DRB. The Septuagint contains more details and different verse numbering. Septuagint translations cited here include the RSVCE and Kata Biblon Wiki English Translation (WET).

The Book of Judith shows the necessity of holding firm confidence in the Virgin Mary. The wise woman of Abel saw that by the death of one man, Sheba, the whole people could be saved. Judith saw the same in beheading Holofernes. Their wisdom lay in identifying the enemy and discerning a way to bring him down while avoiding casualties among the innocent. This is genius. To then carry out the plan successfully requires God's grace and a whole raft of virtues. When it comes to the most formidable enemy on earth, the Antichrist, there is no escape except by Mary, who is full of grace and virtue.[60]

Our wisdom lies in realising God is pleased to rescue us by the hands of a woman and to allow the most humble to bring down the most proud:

> *Then, taking the head of Holofernes from the bag, she displayed it to them, saying: 'Behold, the head of Holofernes the leader of the military of the Assyrians, and behold his canopy, under which he reclined in his drunkenness, where the Lord our God struck him by the hand of a woman.'* (Jud 13:19)

In Judith's story, the Assyrian King Nebuchadnezzar stands for satan inasmuch as he represents that vengeful, remote, ultimate power of evil who gathers all his officers and nobles to explain *"his secret plan"*, a mystery (μυστήριον) emerging from his will, nothing less than *"to subjugate all the earth to*

---

[60] St Louis Marie de Montfort, in *True Devotion to Mary*, writes that the ten principal virtues of the Holy Virgin for our imitation are: her profound humility, lively faith, blind obedience, continual prayer, universal mortification, divine purity, ardent charity, heroic patience, angelical sweetness, and heavenly wisdom.

his authority" (Jud 2:2-3).[61] Arrogantly he styles himself *"the great king, the lord of all the earth"* (Jud 2:5). Unwittingly fitting into an ancient pattern, he appoints his antichrist, *"Holofernes, the chief general of his army, second only to himself"* (Jud 2:4 RSVCE), commissioning him to *"cover the whole face of the earth with the feet of my armies"* (Jud 2:7 RSVCE). Nebuchadnezzar relishes the uncountable deaths his plan should cause and the enslavement of all survivors: *"They will yield themselves to you, and you shall hold them for me till the day of their punishment"* (Jud 2:10 RSVCE).

Holofernes is pleased to follow all the evil instructions of *"his lord"* (Jud 2:15, κύριος). At Mass we call on the true Κύριος for mercy (*Kyrie eleison*), but from the false κύριος there is no mercy. As the bloodbath overflows in neighbouring lands, terrorised populations make a festival of Holofernes' arrival, hoping hopelessly to appease him. But unrelenting:

he demolished all their shrines and cut down their sacred groves; for it had been given to him to destroy all the gods of the land, so that all nations should worship Nebuchadnezzar only, and all their tongues and tribes should call upon him as god. (Jud 3:7-8 RSVCE)[62]

---

[61] From the Septuagint we have: *"decreed the destruction of all flesh, who did not follow the word of his mouth"* (Jud 2:3). This is perfectly totalitarian: to bring all one can subdue under one's control; to destroy everything else; while denying the transcendent even exists. Thoroughly ungodly, Nebuchadnezzar decrees to destroy all flesh (πᾶσαν σάρκα), has his own acolytes (ἠκολούθησαν), and issues his own word (τῷ λόγῳ τοῦ στόματος αὐτοῦ) in contradiction to God's Word, the Logos.

[62] Literally "κατέσκαψεν πάντα τὰ ὅρια αὐτῶν" *"demolished all their borders"*. This warns of the globalist programme involving breaking down national identity.

This is perfectly apocalyptic: the destruction of all the world's religions, the evil one driven to eradicate competition, demanding on pain of death that he alone be worshipped (Apoc 13:12,15). The unlimited ambition, vainglory and pride of the Antichrist make him necessarily a globalist.[63]

All peoples but one collapse in fear before Holofernes, prefiguring the moral paralysis of the last generation, those who ask: *"Who is like the beast? And who can fight against it?"* (Apoc 13:4 RSVCE). All bow to him except Israel, who had just emerged from the major trial of exile:

> *By this time the people of Israel living in Judea heard of everything that Holofernes, the general of Nebuchadnezzar the king of the Assyrians, had done to the nations, and how he had plundered and destroyed all their temples; they were therefore very greatly terrified at his approach, and were alarmed both for Jerusalem and for the temple of the Lord their God. For they had only recently returned from the captivity, and all the people of Judea were newly gathered together, and the sacred vessels and the altar and the temple had been consecrated after their profanation. (Jud 4:1-3 RSVCE)*

If you have ever escaped one cataclysm only to face a new one, the second is perhaps not meant for your destruction, but

---

[63] *"And they worshiped the dragon, who gave authority to the beast. And they worshiped the beast... And it was given to him to make war with the saints and to overcome them. And authority was given to him over every tribe and people and language and nation. And all who inhabit the earth will worship the beast, everyone whose names have not been written from the origin of the world in the Book of Life of the Lamb who was slain"* (Apoc 13:4-8).

the first was given to train you to overcome it. God gives chastisements so that we might stand at the end. Faced by the Assyrian threat, orders go out from Jerusalem from the High Priest and elders (for the actual Apocalypse, here we might read "Rome", "Pope", "Cardinals") for all to fast in sackcloth and pray x(Jud 4:8-9). The Israelites (now "Catholics") obeyed and the fervent prayer of the whole people was heard:

> *So God heard their prayers and looked upon their afflictions; for the people fasted many days in all Judea and Jerusalem before the sanctuary of the Lord Almighty. And Joacim the high priest, and all the priests who stood before the Lord and those who ministered to the Lord, had their loins dressed with sackcloth, and offered the daily burnt offerings* [cf. Holy Mass] *with the vows and free gifts of the people, and had ashes on their liturgical headdresses; and they cried to the Lord with all their power, so that he would look upon all the house of Israel graciously.* (Jud 4:13-15 WET)

Having done *penance! penance! penance!* and prayed with all their heart, the Israelites prepare practically for resistance, fortifying their cities and mountain passes. When this is reported to Holofernes, he is enraged, and asks searching questions over the identity of this people who alone dare to defy him (Jud 5:1-4). Achior the Ammonite explains to him they are distinguished from all other peoples as worshippers of the true God, and that when they return to their traditions after straying, they become indestructible by outside forces. Only their own infidelity can ruin them.

O, that the Church would heed Achior's wisdom and return to her traditions!

> *There was no one who could attack this people, except when they withdrew from the worship of the Lord their God. But as often as they worshipped any other, except their own God, they were delivered to plunder, and to the sword, and into reproach. But as often as they were repentant for having withdrawn from the worship of their God, the God of heaven gave them the power to resist.* (Jud 5:17-19)[64]

O, that the Church would heed Achior's wisdom and root out impurity!

> *As long as they did not sin in the sight of their God, it was well with them... Recently returning to the Lord their God, from the dispersion in which they had been scattered, they have united and have ascended into all these mountains, and they again possess Jerusalem, where their holy things are... If there may be no offence of this people before their God, we will not be able to resist them, because their God will defend them, and we will become a disgrace to the whole earth.* (Jud 5:21-25)

---

[64] Also Antiochus, a later figure of the Antichrist, *"now professed that the Jews had God as their protector, and, for this reason, they were invulnerable, because they followed the laws established by him"* (2 Macc 8:36).

Achior's accurate appraisal was detestable in the ears of Holofernes' Moabite advisors, who indignantly insisted:

We will not be afraid of the faces of the children of Israel, for we see that they are a people who have no strength or power for a strong battle. (Jud 5:23 WET)

In the end times the worldly will not understand the invincible strength of the Church who, when thoroughly purified, is true in her worship. The weakness of the world is not that it is ignorant of Church history, but that it does not hear it with the ears of faith. So Holofernes could not perceive what Achior was trying to tell him. Unmoved by revealed truth, Holofernes in his satanic blasphemy boasts:

who is God but Nebuchadnezzar? He will send his power and will destroy them from the face of the earth and their God will not deliver them; but we, his servants, will destroy them as if they were one man; for they are not able to withstand the power of our horses. For with them, we will tread them under foot, and their mountains will be drunken with their blood and their fields will be filled with their dead bodies and their footsteps will not be able to stand before us, for they will utterly perish, as king Nebuchadnezzar, lord of all the earth, has said:... *'None of my words will be in vain'.* (Jud 6:2-4 WET)

Infatuated by evil, Holofernes echoes the arrogance of his distant master, adding: *"I have spoken and none of my words shall fail"* (Jud 6:9 RSVCE). They were blind to their own Assyrian history. A few centuries before, around 700 BC, their

King Sennacherib besieged Jerusalem, sending letters of contempt to the Jewish King Hezekiah, dismissing the ability of God to deliver His People, and boasting that until now none of the peoples with their gods had been able to withstand him (2 Chron 32:1-23; 2 Kngs 18:13-19:37). He sent servants to read out these letters in the hearing of Jerusalem's defenders, shouting insults in Hebrew and seeking to undermine Jewish morale. But the Most High God confounded Sennacherib's army. Shamefaced, he returned home. Entering the temple of his god, he was cut down dead by that which had issued from his loins, his own sons wielding the swords. King Hezekiah had put his trust in the Lord. Sennacherib's boast came to nothing. Perhaps it was because the Assyrian annals skip over this humiliation that their descendants were bound to experience another? The Jews had more honest history books to learn from, detailing their disastrous infidelities as well as their heroes and the aid of the Living God. Honesty wins.

Courageous like David against Goliath, the men of the most crucial mountain town, Bethulia, resist the approaching Assyrian army with stones from slings (Jud 6:12). They are terrified by the sight of Holofernes' forces but are determined to stand their ground (Jud 7:4-5). Slowly, however, under an iron siege, fading from hunger and thirst, the will of the population fails, and on day thirty-four they call on their leaders to make peace with the beast, even though it will cost them enslavement. The leaders ask them to hold on five days more, saying if God will not intervene before this deadline expires, then they will surrender (Jud 8:19-32).

The plan for surrender was sinful. Were they willing to endure thirty-nine days, but not forty? Their ancestors, waiting for Moses to descend the holy mountain, pressed Aaron to make the Golden Calf on the thirty-ninth day, murmuring: *"as for this Moses, the man who brought us up out of the land of Egypt, we don't know what has become of him"* (Ex 32:23). They ought to have known their Deliverer lives, but they could not bear further delay. It is a warning for the Church not to quit. God exhorts us: *"He who perseveres to the end shall be saved"* (Mt 24:13). Now the whole of Bethulia would have followed this fatal counsel, but as the Church has Mary, so the besieged mountain stronghold had Judith. Thanks to her, the days of trial were shortened (cf. Mt 24:22), and victory came before anyone perished of thirst.

Judith, whose name means Jewess, was a widow of forty months (Jud 8:4 LXX).[65] She had erected a tabernacle on her roof, a sign of her elevated prayer life. She wore haircloth around her waist and fasted all the days of her widowhood, except of course on Israel's feasts. Judith was elegant in appearance, lovely to behold, *"prudent of heart, discerning in judgement, and... virtuous"* (Jud 8:7 RSVCE). From her husband she had inherited tremendous wealth — gold and silver, men and women slaves, cattle and fields — which estate she maintained. All these details we may ponder as even more true of Our Lady, obviously translating the material to

---

[65] The Vulgate has forty-two months, the same symbolic period of the Antichrist's reign (Apoc 11:2,3; 12:6,14; 13:5). When the prescribed time from Christ's Passion has run (the death of Judith's man), then Our Lady will crush the serpent's head.

the spiritual and affirming her slaves are slaves of love. *"And there was no one who spoke an ill word about her, for she feared God greatly"* (Jud 8:8 WET).

Judith rebukes the leaders of Bethulia for putting God to the test. She addresses them with theological insight, discerning divine scourging unto disgrace from divine scourging unto discipline. Given that none of their tribes or cities were now fallen in idolatry, they could have full confidence in God's deliverance. In the past God scourged His people to correct them from infidelity. In this case, *"the Lord scourges those who draw near to him, in order to admonish them"* (Jud 8:27), that is, in order to preach to them, teach them, educate them about Himself: His holiness, His power, His love. Now their test has come and literally everything depends on the inhabitants of Bethulia for:

> *if we are captured all Judea will be captured and our sanctuary will be plundered; [God] will exact of our blood the penalty for its desecration. And the slaughter of our brethren and the captivity of the land and the desolation of our inheritance...* (Jud 8:21-23 RSVCE)

So it would be if we lost the traditional Mass. Judith encourages them:

> *Now therefore, brethren, let us set an example to our brethren, for their lives depend upon us, and the sanctuary and the temple and the altar rest upon us. In spite of everything let us give thanks to the Lord our*

God, who is putting us to the test as he did our forefathers... (Jud 8:24-25 RSVCE)

She exhorts them to remember the testing of Abraham, of Isaac and of Jacob. The Church must remember them too, meditate on their holy lives in order to survive the final trials, recalling the Patriarchs and understanding thereby the Father, Son and Holy Ghost, even the Passion, Resurrection and Ascension (Gen 15:12; 22:12; 28:12). These are the invincible dogmas, powerful enough to keep our faith, hope and charity strong to the end. Praying the Holy Rosary daily keeps these sublime Mysteries alive in our hearts. The Rosary is Marian wisdom.

Bethulia's leaders acknowledge Judith is right, observing:

this is not the first day that your wisdom has been manifested; but from the beginning of your life all the people have recognised your understanding, because the disposition of your heart has been good. (Jud 8:29 WET)

Accordingly, the Virgin Mary has oftentimes been prefigured, manifesting wisdom *"from the beginning"* for those who have eyes to see. The astute leaders ask for her intercession: *"Now, therefore, pray for us, because you are a holy woman, and one fearing God"* (Jud 8:29). Judith responds:

Listen to me and I will do something which will be remembered throughout all generations among the children of our nation... But do not ask me what I will do, for I will not reveal it to you until the things that I do are completed. (Jud 8:32-34)

What Judith carried out has indeed been remembered ever since, throughout all generations. And this is true of the Virgin Mary to a far greater extent. Many have heard of Judith; everyone has heard of Mary. And whereas Judith would not reveal her plans in advance, so it would be futile to speculate before the time comes as to exactly how Mary will crush the serpent's head. The overly curious, lacking humility, fall victim to shameless charlatans who claim to receive special revelations. These latter deserve to be damned, but how tragic that so many follow them into the pit. Instead, we are given enough certain signs — such as at Walsingham, Guadalupe, Lourdes, Fatima — that we ought to listen to Mary, trust her, imitate her, follow her instructions.

Anticipating Mary, Judith, also a widow, humbles herself, uniting her fervent prayer with the evening sacrifice in Jerusalem (Jud 9:1). Similarly we may unite our prayers with those of the whole Church through the liturgy, above all Holy Mass and Vespers. Judith has full confidence in God because she knows Him, because she is familiar with how He has acted in the past:

And you have wrought not only those things, but also the things which happened before and which followed afterwards; you have thought about the things which are now and which are to come. Yes, the things you established were ready at hand, and they said, 'Lo, we are here,' for all your ways are prepared and your judgments are in your foreknowledge. (Jud 9:5-6 WET)

Whoever accepts this will not be surprised to find links running between the Protoevangelium, Jael, the woman in Thebez, Jephthah's daughter, the wise woman in Abel and now Judith, all pointing to the Blessed Virgin Mary. God desires, by using history and the Scriptures, to communicate His ways to those who have ears to hear.

Like Mary with her Magnificat, Judith is zealous for the holiness of God's Name, confidently calling on Him to cast down the mighty and rescue the lowly, to remember His Covenant (Jud 9:7-14; cf. 16:1-17). She asks God to send His wrath down on prideful heads, *"to crush the arrogant by the hands of a woman"* (Jud 9:10 RSVCE). Having prayed, Judith makes practical preparations: bathing, adorning herself with gorgeous clothes and jewellery, giving her maid wine and fine bread to bring with them — allusions to baptism, putting on virtue, and the Holy Eucharist.[66]

Strikingly dressed and radiant with holiness, Judith descends to the Assyrian camp, dazzling the enemy:

And when the men had heard her words, they beheld her face, and their eyes were astounded, because they wondered exceedingly at her beauty. (Jud 10:14)

Suspecting no danger, they take her to Holofernes. Judith flatters him with apparent praise, but in fact she is calling out the arrogance and cruel control-freakery which pervade the

---

[66] Judith instructed her maid to bring "ἄρτων καθαρῶν" (Jud 10:5), meaning pure bread, echoing in Greek the *"clean"* animals suitable to be sacrificed and consumed (cf. Gen 7:2; 8:20; Lev 11:47; 20:25).

operations of Nebuchadnezzar and his chief agent Holofernes, foreshadowing the operations of satan and his Antichrist:

> *Nebuchadnezzar the king of the whole earth lives, and as his power endures, who had sent you to direct every living soul, not only do men serve him because of you, but also the beasts of the field and the cattle and the birds of the air will live by your power under Nebuchadnezzar and all his house.* (Jud 11:7 RSVCE)

How grotesque that anyone but Christ be sent *"to direct every living soul"*; how grotesque that anyone but the Father be the origin of such an encompassing mission; how grotesque that the words *"men serve him because of you"* should apply to Nebuchadnezzar and Holofernes as a foreshadowing of satan and the Antichrist, rather than the Father and Son. It ought only be that men worship the Triune God thanks to the revelation and self-sacrifice of Jesus, but the final perversion will be the worship of satan thanks to the deceit and threats of the Antichrist. How grotesque that the life of *"the beasts of the field and the cattle and the birds of the air"* be attributed not to the Creator but to a mortal, Holofernes, one who must die, and will soon die. Likewise, the Antichrist will be praised for preternatural powers he has received from satan, though both of them will end up dying for eternity in the pit.

Continuing this spiritual interpretation of Judith's words, what she said next, whether a ruse at the time or factually true, applies to the future Church; namely, the Church's temptation to self-degradation, manifested in recent decades, but which must be corrected if the Church is to withstand the final persecutions and trials:

> *our nation cannot be punished, nor can the sword prevail against them, unless they sin against their God... Since their food supply is exhausted and their water has almost given out, they have planned to kill their cattle and have determined to use all that God by his laws has forbidden them to eat. They have decided to consume the first fruits of the grain and the tithes of the wine and oil, which they had consecrated and set aside for the priests who minister in the presence of our God at Jerusalem — although it is not lawful for any of the people so much as to touch these things with their hands. They have sent men to Jerusalem, because even the people living there have been doing this, to bring back to them permission from the senate. When the word reaches them and they proceed to do this, on that very day they will be handed over to you to be destroyed.* (Jud 11:10-15 RSVCE)

Judith found it deplorable that the people should touch with their hands the consecrated grain and tithes of wine and oil. This is a warning to the Church that, in the desperation of being besieged, she must not accommodate herself to the world. She must not despise her holy things, nor allow people to receive the Blessed Sacrament in their hands. If the OT signs of grain and wine were too holy to touch, how much more the sacramental reality of Christ's Body and Blood? Catholics see Lutherans, Anglicans and Calvinists taking bits of bread from each other and scattering the crumbs on the ground, passing around cupfuls of wine and even pouring the excess down the drain. Feeling besieged, Catholics have cowered, adopting an alien theology of symbology, copying heretical ways. Except Protestants are handling only bread, while Catholics mistreat the real Body of Christ.

Judith knew such sacrilege in Bethulia would mean the fall of all Israel. God had called them to hold out, even though Jerusalem in weakness was willing to grant *"permission from the senate"*. It would be as if priests at traditional Masses were willing to give Holy Communion in the hand. If they do, it is all over. Even if Jerusalem (the Vatican) has stumbled, Bethulia (Tradition) must not.

Those who think the Old Covenant was abolished by Jesus rather than fulfilled will think this is an overreaction. But the spiritual consequences of violating the New Covenant are worse than the physical punishment for profaning the Old. During the Babylonian exile, the King's son Belshazzar made a stupendous feast and ordered that the precious vessels of gold and silver, which his father King Nebuchadnezzar had stolen from the Temple in Jerusalem, be used to give wine to his noble guests, his wives and his concubines. Doing this they praised false gods.

> *Immediately the fingers of a man's hand appeared and wrote on the plaster of the wall of the king's palace, opposite the lampstand... Then the king's colour changed, and his thoughts alarmed him; his limbs gave way, and his knees knocked together.* (Dan 5:5-6 RSVCE)

He was right to fear. But why do they not fear, those sons of the Roman Curia, who have given permission for laity to take in their unconsecrated hands the precious chalice of the Lord's Blood? Do they not think the consecration of hands during the rite of priestly ordination makes any difference? The faithless count sacerdotal consecration as clericalism. But do they not pause when they read of Daniel giving God's judgement on Belshazzar for treating lightly the ancient vessels which held only water, wine or the blood of animals:

> *[You], Belshazzar, have not humbled your heart, though you knew all this, but you have lifted up yourself against the Lord of heaven; and the vessels of his house have been brought in before you, and you and your lords, your wives, and your concubines have drunk wine from them; and you have praised the gods of silver and gold... which do not see or hear or know, but the God in whose hand is your breath, and whose are all your ways, you have not honoured.* (Dan 5:22-23 RSVCE)

What proportion is there here with chalices for the Blood of God made Man? Why do our ecclesial princes not read this and tremble? *"That very night Belshazzar the Chaldean king was slain"* (Dan 5:30 RSVCE). We are warned of what is at stake by Judith, who described next the calamity that would happen if her people in Bethulia fell into sin. Thanks be to God they did not, so Judith's conditional prediction never came about, but it remains a warning to us of what will happen if our liturgical reverence grows cold, if we treat as profane that matter offered to the Lord:

> *God has sent me to accomplish with you things that will astonish the whole world, as many as shall hear about them. For your servant is religious, and serves the God of heaven day and night... [W]hen they have committed their sins... I will lead you through the middle of Judea, till you come to Jerusalem; and I will set your throne in the midst of it; and you will lead them like sheep that have no shepherd, and not a dog will so much as open its mouth to growl at you. For this has been told me, by my foreknowledge; it was announced to me, and I was sent to tell you.* (Jud 11:16-19 RSVCE)

The implication here is that if the Church does not hold pure, or rather if her last defensive communities succumb like their leaders, then the Antichrist will be able to set his throne in Jerusalem (Rome), whose people would be as if without a shepherd (pope). Judith's admonition is crystal clear. Thanks be to God, and to the power He has given to Mary to care for us, the Church is indefectible. Much more than Judith, Mary *"will astonish the whole world"*. In this light, we see Holofernes replies truly, yet with profound ignorance of what is actually unfolding:

> *There is not such a woman from one end of the earth to the other, either for beauty of face or wisdom of speech! ...if you do as you have said, your God shall be my God.* (Jud 11:21-23 RSVCE)

Bound for failure, as the Antichrist seeks to lead the Church astray through false worship, so Holofernes beseeches Judith to share a godless table with him:

Then he commanded them to bring her in where his silver dishes were kept, and ordered them to set a table for her with some of his own food and to serve her with his own wine. But Judith said, 'I cannot eat it, lest it be an offence; but I will be provided from the things I have brought with me.' (Jud 12:1-2 RSVCE)

Our Lady is not pleased by ecumenical 'worship' which confounds her Son's Real Presence on the altar with mere bread and wine on a table. Despite all attacks on Holy Mass, let us be sure like Judith that God will provide unto the end:

Judith replied, 'As your soul lives, my lord, your servant will not use up the things I have with me before the Lord carries out by my hand what he has determined to do.' (Jud 12:4 RSVCE)

The Church is to retain her own pure worship (Jud 12:8-9), swallowing up the Antichrist (Jud 13:9-10). Never suspecting a humble woman could be his nemesis, Holofernes lays on a banquet, intending to violate Judith at the end of it. Eventually the assembled generals, counsellors, guards and servants all leave: *"So Judith was left alone in the tent, with Holofernes stretched out on his bed, for he was overcome with wine"* (Jud 13:2 RSVCE).

And Judith stood in front of the bed, praying with tears, and her lips moved in silence, saying: 'Confirm me, O Lord God of Israel, and in this hour look kindly upon the works of my hands, so that, just as you promised, you may raise up Jerusalem, your city, and so that, believing through you that this plan is able to be accomplished, I may succeed'... and [unsheathing] his blade... she struck him twice on his neck, and she cut off his head. (Jud 13:6-10)

The first stroke represents the prefigurations, the second stroke the decisive conclusion. The enemy is decapitated by his own blade (Russia?). The immediate reaction in Bethulia, when Judith returns, is for all to bow down worshipping God (Jud 13:17), calling Him *"blessed"*. Then the leaders call Judith *"blessed"* with words which are more true for Mary:

O daughter, you are blessed by the Most High God above all women on earth; and blessed be the Lord God, who created the heavens and the earth, who has guided you to strike the head of the leader of our enemies. Your hope will never depart from the hearts of men, as they remember the power of God. May God grant this to be a perpetual honour to you, and may he visit you with blessings... (Jud 13:18-20 RSVCE)

To this the people answer: *"Amen"*. Achior unknowingly alludes to the Hail Mary and Magnificat:

Blessed art thou by thy God in every tabernacle of Jacob, for in every nation which shall hear thy name,

the God of Israel shall be magnified on occasion of thee.
(Jud 13:31 DRB)[67]

On Judith's instructions, the whole enemy army is routed (Jud 14:1-15:7), crying, *"The slaves have tricked us! One Hebrew woman has brought disgrace upon the house of King Nebuchadnezzar!"* (Jud 14:18 RSVCE). With one voice the High Priest and elders of Jerusalem declare of their Jewess:

'You are the glory of Jerusalem, you are the joy of Israel, you are the honour of our people... For you loved chastity... Therefore also the hand of the Lord has strengthened you, and, therefore, you will be blessed for all eternity.' And all the people said: 'Amen. Amen.'
(Jud 15:10-12)

With similar words, Rome and her saints honour Mary.[68] As the enthusiastic reaction of the whole people indicates, the Christian faithful are pleased to honour Mary in devotions, in crownings, in liturgy (Jud 15:12-13; 16:18-20). By God's grace, a woman's virtue saved the day: her wisdom, beauty, humility and courage.

---

[67] Achior converts: *"he believed God, and circumcised the flesh of his foreskin, and was joined to the people of Israel, with all the succession of his kindred until this present day"* (Jud 14:6 DRB). He becomes a son of Abraham through spiritual circumcision, his reward for unashamedly speaking the truth about God and Hebrew history to the antichrist's face, unintimidated, and for enduring a type of Crucifixion: *"by the side of the mountain, they tied Achior, hands and feet, to a tree, and so they abandoned him... and they returned to their lord"* (Jud 6:9).

[68] The Gradual for the Feast of the Immaculate Conception is from Jud 15:10, *Tu gloria Ierusalem, tu lætitia Israël, tu honorificentia populi nostri. Alleluia, alleluia.*

- *Wisdom* not in the sense of mastering political or military stratagems, although Judith and the Jewish leaders were no fools in appraising these realities. Rather the wisdom that fears God (Jud 16:16), knows God, that depends upon Him entirely, preferring to die than to dishonour Him.
- *Beauty* not like that over which the world drools, but one evoking reverence through chastity. Judith disarmed an entire army with her femininity (Jud 10:14-23) and was not polluted (Jud 13:16). Womanliness defeats the devil. Hence he is the source of that feminism which for over a century has dissolved the differences between men and women, resulting now in the tragic epidemic of gender dysphoria. As balm for recovery, Judith shows no worldly power is a match for a woman being a woman.[69]
- *Humility* not in shrinking or underrating oneself (which might be an excuse to ignore God's power acting through frail instruments), but in depending on God and carrying oneself with modesty, even appearing unthreatening in the eyes of the enemy.[70]
- *Courage* not only in the strength to strike the decisive blow, but in the stamina of never giving up under siege, and in the three days of cool courage going in and out of the enemy camp without breaking a sweat.

These virtues all find their vertex in the Virgin Mother of God.

---

[69] cf. III Esdras 4:13-34, an extra-canonical text relating Zorobabel's entertaining yet profound presentation to the court of King Darius.

[70] Also Jael acted graciously to her enemy (Jdg 5:25); and for the kill, she approached *"softly"* (Jdg 4:21).

The High Priest Joacim came from Jerusalem to Bethulia with all his elders and praised Judith for having *"done all this singlehanded"* (Jud 15:10 RSVCE). In a sense this is true: Judith was key. But lest anyone accuse Catholics of idolatry in claiming Mary achieves all, for her part Judith like Mary gives all the glory to God, recognising it was He Who defeated the enemies, even by her hand.[71]

Moreover, Judith powerfully exhorted the leaders and people to play their part. The success of the whole operation depended on the people of Bethulia following her instructions and not falling into sin, into sacrilege, but enduring to the end.[72] Thus Christians are right to call with confidence upon the assistance of the Blessed Virgin Mary, even unto the defeat of the Antichrist, but we must do so with purity of faith and great perseverance. To fulfil God's plan, to avoid His punishment, the remnant — Bethulia — may not fail.

Who, then, are the inhabitants of Bethulia? The name means 'Yahweh's Virgin', which most suitably anticipates the Virgin Mary.[73] The inhabitants are those of Mary's city: they trust her, follow her instructions, they are her devotees.[74] Perhaps her faithful maid, who accompanied Judith all the way into the enemy camp, and in her daily prayers, and

---

[71] Jud 9:7-8,14; 13:4-5,11,14; 16:3,6,13,17 (RSVCE).

[72] Jud 8:11-27,32-34; 10:9; 11:10-19; 13:11; 14:1-5 (RSVCE).

[73] בְּתוּלָה (Betulah) is virgin. The ending, יה (Yah) is the abbreviated Name of God, יהוה (YHWH). A complementary derivation is from בֵּית־אֵל (Beth-el) which means 'House of God' (cf. Gen 28:16,19). The Church is both House of God and also God's Virgin.

[74] Jud 15:12-13; 16:11-12 (RSVCE).

worked in her service, represents those who make a total consecration to Mary? Like Judith, such consecrations are becoming *"more and more famous"*, and in the end, Judith *"set her maid free"* (Jud 16:23 RSVCE). So those who consecrate themselves as slaves of love to Jesus through Mary discover the truest type of freedom: adhesion to God's Will. These are the ones who stay true to the ancient traditions, maintaining traditional worship: these have the high ground, the mountains, but are few in number and live out on the peripheries, the border, far from the centres of power. These are hungry and thirsty and suffer the brunt of the enemy's assault. But they must endure. We must endure. This fidelity and service — this slavery — liberates us from the enemy.

Waiting for the Mother of God to defeat the Antichrist cannot be an excuse for quietism or retreat. Rather, through Judith, the Virgin Mary calls for our holiness and devotion and fidelity and final perseverance.

QUEEN ESTHER: INTERCESSOR FOR HER PEOPLE

O Lord, do not surrender thy sceptre to what has no being; and do not let them mock at our downfall; but turn their plan against [them], and make an example of the man who began this against us. Remember, O Lord; make thyself known in this time of our affliction, and give me courage, O King of the gods and Master of all dominion! Put eloquent speech in my mouth before the lion, and turn his heart to hate the man who is fighting against us, so that there may be an end of him and those who agree with him. But save us by thy hand...

— Est 14:11-14 [75]

The Book of Esther warns about the end times:

Behold, noise and confusion, thunders and earthquake, tumult upon the earth! And behold, two great dragons came forward, both ready to fight, and they roared terribly. And at their roaring every nation prepared for war, to fight against the nation of the righteous. And behold, a day of darkness and gloom, tribulation and distress, affliction and great tumult upon the earth! And the whole righteous nation was troubled; they feared the evils that threatened them, and were ready to perish. (Est 11:5-9)

---

[75] All Bible references in this chapter refer to the RSVCE unless otherwise noted. Verses from chapters 11 to 16 of the Book of Esther do not appear in the Hebrew Tanakh or Protestant Bibles but are included in the Septuagint and the Vulgate, belonging to the Catholic Canon. Meanwhile chapters 1 to 10 are received by all.

The righteous nation is threatened with extinction. The apocalyptic sense is heightened when we read that the most powerful ruler in the world, in the name of unity and peace, decrees a ferocious persecution against believers, as if these are the only obstacle to the utopian one world order. The genocidal plan was engineered by the insidious lies of Haman who, having attained

> *the second place in the kingdom, pointed out to us that among all the nations in the world there is scattered a certain hostile people, who have laws contrary to those of every nation and continually disregard the ordinances of the kings, so that the unifying of the kingdom which we honourably intend cannot be brought about. We understand that this people, and it alone, stands constantly in opposition to all men, perversely following a strange manner of life and laws, and is ill-disposed to our government, doing all the harm they can so that our kingdom may not attain stability.* (Est 13:3-5)

As the Jews were framed with deadly lies by Haman, so Christians will be scapegoated by the Antichrist:

> *Therefore we have decreed that those indicated to you in the letters of Haman, who is in charge of affairs… shall all, with their wives and children, be utterly destroyed by the sword of their enemies, without pity or mercy… and leave our government completely secure and untroubled hereafter.* (Est 13:6-7)

This is what the Church may expect in the last days: being set apart because of religion; being resented, suspected, falsely accused of threatening the peace and stability of the prevailing order; a violent persecution.

Letters were sent by couriers to all the king's provinces, to destroy, to slay, and to annihilate all Jews, young and old, women and children, in one day, the thirteenth day of the twelfth month... (Est 3:13)

In this historical prefiguration of the end times, thankfully the Persian King Ahasuerus finally acknowledges that he had been deceived by Haman, pointing out how godless men subvert government. His appraisal is very contemporary:

carried away by the boasts of those who know nothing of goodness, they suppose that they will escape the evil-hating justice of God, who always sees everything. And often many of those who are set in places of authority have been made in part responsible for the shedding of innocent blood, and have been involved in irremediable calamities, by the persuasion of friends who have been entrusted with the administration of public affairs, when these men by the false trickery of their evil natures beguile the sincere good will of their sovereigns. What has been wickedly accomplished through the pestilent behaviour of those who exercise authority unworthily, can be seen not so much from the more ancient records which we hand on as from investigation of matters close at hand. (Est 16:4-7)

The King indicates that is profitable to pay heed to the past, and still more necessary to be alert to the present. We should pay attention. Government is a great good of nature, ordained by God. Precisely because of its goodness, it brings honour upon its ministers. This tremendous honour attracts the vainglorious, they who boast, who know nothing of goodness, but with pestilent behaviour exercise authority unworthily. All this was evident 2,500 years ago to Persian historians and observers. Governmental corruption is written into a fallen world, and the Bible advises us to expect it to reach a critical state in the end times.

Despite unavoidable imperfections in the comparison, we may take King Ahasuerus (Artaxerxes) in the Book of Esther as figuring the highest being, God. He *"reigned from India to Ethiopia over one hundred twenty-seven provinces"* (Est 1:1), basically ruling everywhere. As God is ministered to by seven archangels who may enter His presence,[76] so Ahasuerus was served by *"the seven princes of Persia and Media, who saw the king's face, and sat first in the kingdom"* (Est 1:14).

Queen Vashti figures Eve, the woman who lost the favour of the king (God), thereby impending a loss on all (Est 1:18). Esther, as the new Queen, the new Eve, undoes this knot.[77] In the following passage, Esther provides an image of the Virgin Mary already assumed into Heaven and crowned as Queen.

---

[76] *"I am Raphael, one of the seven holy angels who present the prayers of the saints and enter into the presence of the glory of the Holy One"* (Tob 12:15).

[77] Esther, in Hebrew Hadassah (Est 2:7) means myrtle tree. Strikingly pretty, it is an aromatic shrub which blooms with star-like flowers, an evergreen unhurt by the seasons, yielding sweet berries good to eat or, better, for distilling strong liqueur.

The banquet is for the saints in Heaven, while the benefits in the provinces are as graces poured out upon the world:

Now Esther found favour in the eyes of all who saw her... the king loved Esther more than all the women, and she found grace and favour in his sight more than all the virgins, so he set the royal crown on her head and made her queen instead of Vashti. Then the king gave a great banquet to all his princes and servants; it was Esther's banquet. He also granted a remission of taxes to the provinces and gave gifts with royal liberality. (Est 2:15-18)

It was Esther who played the key role in averting the genocide which threatened her people. She succeeded thanks to her various virtues, including piety, obedience, courage, compassion, determination and patience. Due to her beauty Esther was chosen to be introduced to the king and, due to her simplicity, he preferred her above all others (Est 2:2-9,12-17). Her simplicity was fierce:

I hate the glory of the wicked, and I detest the bed of the uncircumcised, and of all outsiders... I loathe the sign of my exaltation and glory, which is on my head in the days of my exhibition, and that I detest it like a menstruous rag and do not wear it in the days of my silence, and that I have not eaten at Haman's table... (Est 8:15-17 SB)

Incorruptible, Esther did not insinuate herself into the royal courts for the sake of glory and prestige, power and luxuries. Rather she was selected by the king for her qualities, which were given her by God in order that she could accomplish her mission. God equips those whom He sends. We may think of Mary being immaculately conceived for her greater mission.

Like Mary, Esther counts herself God's *"handmaid"* and exults in Him alone:

> *And your handmaid has never rejoiced, from the time that I was carried here until this very day, except in you, Lord, God of Abraham.* (Est 8:15-18 SB)

Effectively alone, though communicating with Mordecai, Esther formulated a plan which she executed with cool patience and decisiveness (Est 5:3-8; 6:14; 7:1-10).[78] At a deeper level, by her prayers Esther prefigures Our Lady, both as highly favoured intercessor present in the Courts of Heaven but before that in the pain of Calvary:

> *when she had put aside her royal apparel, she took up garments suitable for weeping and mourning, and instead of various ointments, she covered her head with ashes from burnt dung, and she humbled her body with fasting, and all the aspects of her beauty, she covered with her torn hair.* (Est 8:2 SB)

The soul who humbles herself is exalted (Prov 29; Mt 23:12). The prayer Esther offered up is immaculate (Est 14:1-19). For three days and nights she led a fast for all her people in the

---

[78] Esther was obedient to her adopted father and benefactor Mordecai, maintaining total silence about her Jewish background until the right moment came to reveal it (Est 2:10,20; 7:3-4; 8:5-6). Similarly, Mary was never vainglorious in her unique privileges and did not let the devil discover her Immaculate Conception or divine motherhood until it was too late for him to change his hopeless attack on her Son.

city (Est 4:16). Moved by compassion for her people, Esther was willing to risk her life to save them, for it could be death to approach the king unsummoned (Est 4:11,16).[79] Accepting enormous responsibility and *"majestically adorned"*, she approached, as it were, the very throne of Heaven — such is the force of the description (Est 15:1-16). Without Esther's intervention, all the Jews would have been wiped out. So necessary is Our Blessed Lady's aid for the final struggles of the Church.[80]

The times were evil. Personifying malice, Haman was granted leave to come before the king as satan was permitted to come before God (Job 1:6-12; 2:1-7). Haman, honoured like Lucifer with a high position, aggrandised himself and sought to be worshipped:

King Ahasuerus promoted Haman... and set his seat above all the princes who were with him. And all the king's servants who were at the king's gate bowed down and did obeisance to Haman... (Est 3:1-2)

These princes were unworthy of their positions. Sycophancy ruins government, for the powerful need to be surrounded by souls strong enough to challenge them when they are tempted

---

[79] This may seem severe, but it is true for us in respect to Holy Communion: those who approach the divine Majesty without discernment will die.

[80] The Mother of God's assistance is needful in the final struggle of every soul, so we pray fifty times in the decades of a daily Rosary: *ora pro nobis peccatoribus, nunc et in hora mortis nostrae. Amen.* Indeed we can be more certain of Mary than Mordecai was of Esther, who asked of her: *"And who knows whether you have not come to the kingdom for such a time as this?"* (Est 4:14)

to wield power unjustly. Happily, one man can bring them down. Like Jesus refusing to worship satan (Mt 4:9-10):

But Mordecai did not bow down or do obeisance... Haman was filled with fury. But he disdained to lay hands on Mordecai alone... Haman sought to destroy all the Jews, the people of Mordecai. (Est 3:2-6)

Seething in his pride, this rejection meant Haman could not be content or enjoy his vast powers, honours and riches: *"Yet all this does me no good, so long as I see Mordecai the Jew sitting at the king's gate"* (Est 5:13). He had a huge gibbet erected, fifty cubits high, for Mordecai's execution (Est 5:14). The Septuagint describes it simply as ξύλον and the Vulgate as *excelsam crucem*, which can be fittingly translated as a *"tree"* and a *"high cross"* (Est 9:30 SB cf. 12:7; 14:25 SB). The Book states that two criminals, Bigthana and Teresh, *"were both hanged on a tree"* (Est 2:23 WET). But in this story, it would not be the hero Mordecai who was crucified like them, but his enemy, Haman himself. Jesus' Crucifixion between the two thieves was in fact the defeat of evil, the death of death.

By the terms of his own scheming, everything which Haman sought for himself he was then compelled to award to Mordecai, and exactly the evil he intended for Mordecai he would himself experience (Est 6:7-11).[81] This is perfect

---

[81] Precisely when Haman was poised for final triumph, the king was prompted by a dream to examine the chronicles and memories of the past, and thereby realised what a godsend and saviour Mordecai was (Est 6:1-3). This may stand for a timely divine intervention in the end times so key players discover our Saviour, Jesus Christ, in the old records, that is the OT.

justice. Haman's hopes began collapsing. Queen Esther, irresistible in her majesty, asked the King to spare her and her people from treacherous genocide:

> *'This is our most wicked enemy and foe: Haman!'*
> *Hearing this, Haman was suddenly dumbfounded, unable to*
> *bear the faces of the king and the queen.* (Est 11:6 SB)

One who cannot see the face of God or Mary loses their own, loses their life:

> *and immediately they covered his face. And Harbona,*
> *one of the eunuchs who stood in ministry to the king,*
> *said, 'Behold the wood, which he had prepared for*
> *Mordecai, who spoke up on behalf of the king, stands in*
> *Haman's house, having a height of fifty cubits.' The king*
> *said, 'Hang him from it.' And so Haman was hanged on*
> *the gallows, which he had prepared for Mordecai, and*
> *the king's anger was quieted.* (Est 11:8-10 SB)

That Haman was hung on his own scaffold demonstrates that evil consumes itself: *"Finally, both he and his sons were fastened to a cross"* (Est 14:25 SB).[82] This is not the poetic touch of a storyteller, but the metaphysical fabric of reality. Countless stories and verses in the OT insist that evil eventually comes back to fall on the head of its instigator.[83]

---

[82] Moreover, Haman's house was given to Queen Esther, who set Mordecai over it (Est 12:1-2 SB; cf. Mt 25:28-30).

[83] Prov 1:18 *"they lie in ambush against their own blood, and they undertake deceits against their own souls"*. Also 1 Sam 25:39; 1 Kngs 2:32,44; 2 Chron 6:23; Ps 7:16-17; 36:12-15; 56:7; 93:23; Prov 13:6,13,15; 14:1,32; 26:26-27; Eccl 10:8-9; Is 3:10-11; Ezek 9:10; 11:21; 22:31; 35:15; Joel 3:7; Obad 1:15.

Note that time had to be allowed for Haman to work his way up toward the summit of power, to build the scaffold, to lobby for the genocidal decree. Thus evil develops its plans, putting the good under threat of death. The measure of sins must be filled up, which for feeble humans takes centuries (Gen 6:13; 15:16; 2 Macc 6:14; Mt 23:32; 1 Thes 2:16). God does not intervene so as to revoke free will. Such would not merely be taking back a gift, but undoing the very nature of His highest creatures, angels and men, implying — *per impossibile* — that God had erred in our creation.[84] Rather God strengthens His saints to bear all up to the point where evil goes so far as to destroy itself.[85] In Esther's time, an edict was sent out forestalling the threatened evil by one day:

The king commanded them to bring together the Jews throughout each city, and to instruct them to join together, so as to make a stand for their lives, and to execute and destroy all their enemies, with their wives and children and their entire houses, and to plunder their spoil. And one day of retribution was established throughout all the provinces, namely, the thirteenth of the twelfth month Adar. (Est 12:11-12 SB)

---

[84] An edict of the King of the Persians and Medes cannot be revoked (Est 1:19; 8:8; Dan 6:8). How much more the divine decrees and gifts are not retracted.

[85] This way is perfect. It shows God restrains Himself, showing mercy in giving each person time to repent of their sins. Further, it proves the charity of His saints, who endure everything that evil can throw at them. And finally, it demonstrates the inevitable futility of opposing God. Hence we should be as patient under persecution as Christ crucified, for God is always in control, deserving our full trust. He is never confounded, nor are those who put their hope in Him.

The Jews were highly active in achieving their own deliverance while also being fully dependent, in different ways, on Ahasuerus, Mordecai and Esther. So, in a threefold parallel, Christians attain salvation by cooperating with the call to God, through Jesus, in Mary.

All the Jews in Susa, following Esther and Mordecai, made a strict three-day fast. Such *Penance! Penance! Penance!* is the wish Our Lady expressed at Lourdes and Fatima. Significantly, Our Lady of Fatima wore the Star of Esther on her dress when appearing to the shepherd children (in Persian Esther means "star", from *stāra*). Her call to penance is a preparation for the final confrontation of God's People and their enemies. Foreshadowing this in Esther's day, the Jews prepared spiritually, and on the order, acted decisively. The description of their deeds anticipates the power of Jesus' Name, the spread of His Gospel, the sword of His Word:

> *Likewise, the fame of his name increased daily and flew everywhere through word of mouth. And so the Jews struck their enemies like a great plague and killed them, repaying according to what they had prepared to do to them, so much so that even in Susa they executed five hundred men, besides the ten sons of Haman the Agagite, the enemy of the Jews.* (Est 14:5-6 SB)

This represents in the New Covenant not murderous, vengeful violence, but a spiritual slaughter of sin. What remains valid is that the instrument of the wicked is turned against them and the moment of execution also: the day they plotted to be the destruction of the good, becomes their own destruction. Had they not plotted, they would not have suffered. Had they not devised a weapon against the good, nothing could have turned against them. They imagined the thirteenth day of the twelfth month would be their triumph, but these figures belong to Our Lady and the Apostles, and the ultimate triumph too.

To establish a perpetual remembrance of this event, the Feast of Purim was inaugurated:

> *For God, who rules over all things, has made this day to be a joy to his chosen people instead of a day of destruction for them.* (Est 16:21)

God declares His Plan, a consolation to those who have faith, and a rebuke to those who do not:

> *Therefore you shall observe this with all good cheer as a notable day among your commemorative festivals, so that both now and hereafter it may mean salvation for us and the loyal Persians, but that for those who plot against us it may be a reminder of destruction.* (Est 16:22-23)

Christians do not keep this feast because, ever since the Crucifixion, it is not apt to celebrate slaughter. But we ought never to forget the Book of Esther. Among other truths, it teaches that if we abandon the Faith we will be subjugated by our enemies; and their apocalyptic aim is to wipe out true religion and Holy Mass:

And now we have sinned before thee, and thou hast given us into the hands of our enemies, because we glorified their gods. Thou art righteous, O Lord! And now they are not satisfied that we are in bitter slavery, but they have covenanted with their idols to abolish what thy mouth has ordained and to destroy thy inheritance, to stop the mouths of those who praise thee and to quench thy altar and the glory of thy house, to open the mouths of the nations for the praise of vain idols, and to magnify for ever a mortal king. O Lord, do not surrender thy sceptre to what has no being; and do not let them mock at our downfall; but turn their plan against themselves, and make an example of the man who began this against us. (Est 14:6-11)

How they loved God! Their infidelity had brought them low, but in misery they discovered that God alone is good. Even His punishments are good, and what zeal they awaken. The more evil appears to succeed in fighting against the one, the true, the good and the beautiful, the more it reveals itself to be chaotic, insane, harmful and ugly. Simultaneously it causes us to yearn for the indivisible and immense splendour of the eternal, to seek the Face of God. How absurd is evil! Privation declaring war against the Transcendent; that which is less than zero pitting itself against the fullness of reality. *"O Lord, do not surrender thy sceptre to what has no being."* Of course He will not. If we do not have the metaphysics or religious sense to appreciate this, we can gain exactly the same truth on the human level from the story of Esther and Mordecai.

Mordecai, within inevitable limits, prefigures Jesus Christ. We note that as Jesus was obedient to Mary (Lk 2:51), so Mordecai also *"did everything as Esther had ordered him"* (Est 4:17). Like Jesus, Mordecai was put to the test, the tempter asking to be worshipped. He prayed:

> *Thou knowest all things; thou knowest, O Lord, that it was not in insolence or pride or for any love of glory that I did this, and refused to bow down to this proud Haman. For I would have been willing to kiss the soles of his feet, to save Israel! But I did this, that I might not set the glory of man above the glory of God, and I will not bow down to any one but to thee, who art my Lord.* (Est 13:12-14 DRB)

How perfectly Christlike to be willing to die rather than set the glory of man above God. How profoundly wise was Mordecai, one in a million, in realising he could not serve his people by showing subservience to evil, but only by resisting it, no matter the cost. The guarantee of this is God Himself. So even when wood was erected for Mordecai's execution, he lived. The highest power, Ahasuerus, praises him as *"saviour"*:

> *[Haman] with intricate craft and deceit asked for the destruction of Mordecai, our saviour and perpetual benefactor, and of Esther, the blameless partner of our kingdom, together with their whole nation.* (Est 16:13)

Mordecai achieved his work through Esther, as Jesus is pleased to make Mary Co-Redemptrix. We may hope the pope, acting as Vicar of Christ, will proclaim this Marian dogma. Then he through Him may beg her to intercede for the people:

Remembering the days of your lowliness, when you were cared for by me... Beseech the Lord and speak to the king concerning us and deliver us from death. (Est 4:8)

Thanks to her intercession, the king's final judgment on those threatened by Haman anticipates what will be the judgement of history on Christians threatened by the Antichrist:

We find that the Jews, who were consigned to annihilation by this thrice accursed man, are not evildoers but are governed by most righteous laws and are sons of the Most High, the most mighty living God. (Est 16:15-16)

As a summary of the hidden meaning of the whole Book, the Catholic Canon (though not the Jewish or Protestant Scriptures) includes Mordecai's reflections on his apocalyptic dream. The passage is worth reading and re-reading with the following key: Artaxerxes (Ahasuerus) representing God; Mordecai representing Jesus, elevated to God's Right Hand; Esther representing Mary Mother of God; Israel as the Church; the second dragon as satan; the day of *"lots"* as Judgement Day:

Truly, king Artaxerxes made all the land, and all the islands of the sea, tributaries. And his strength and his authority, and the dignity and supremacy with which he exalted Mordecai, have been written in the books of the

Medes and the Persians, and how Mordecai of Jewish birth, was second after king Artaxerxes, and great among the Jews, and acceptable to the people of his brethren, seeking the good of his people, and speaking about things which pertained to peace for their descendants. And Mordecai said, 'By God have these things been done. I remember a dream that I saw, which signified these same things, and nothing of this whatsoever has failed to occur. The little fountain which grew into a river, and had turned into light and into the sun, and overflowed into many waters, is Esther, whom the king received as wife and whom he preferred to be queen. But the two dragons are I and Haman. The peoples who gathered together are those who had attempted to erase the name of the Jews. And my people is Israel, who cried out to the Lord, and the Lord brought salvation to his people, and he freed us from all evils, and he created great signs and portents among the nations. And he commanded there to be two lots, one for the people of God and the other for all the nations. And both lots arrived at the day appointed before God, even from that past time, for all peoples. And the Lord remembered his people and had mercy on his inheritance'. (Est 15:1-12 SB)

If we want to be braced for the end times, a careful reading of Esther provides guidance and gives hope against hope.

Inerrantly, Mordecai tells us that the river and the light of his dream is Esther. As objects can represent a person, then

110

with a livelier congruence, persons can represent other persons. Esther represents Mary. St Bonaventure tells us:

> Mary the Queen is also the distributrix of grace. This is indicated in the Book of Esther, where it is said: *'The little spring which grew into a river and was turned into a light and into the sun'*. The Virgin Mary, under the type of Esther, is compared to the outpouring of a spring and of light, because of the diffusion of grace for two uses, that is, for action and for contemplation. For the grace of God, which is a healing for the human race, descends to us through her as if through an aqueduct, since the dispensing of grace is attributed to the Virgin not as to its beginning, but because of her position through merit. By position the Virgin Mary is a most excellent Queen toward her people: she obtains forgiveness, overcomes strife, distributes grace, and thereby she leads them to glory.[86]

These signs of the spring and the light appeared at Lourdes and Fatima, the healing waters and the astounding sun. As St Bonaventure noted six hundred years in advance, the water stands for grace. The radiating light in which Our Lady is dressed is one with the sun, the light of Christ. So the Virgin Mother proclaims the truth about Jesus and leads us to glory.

The Franciscan *doctor seraphicus* wrote truly "the Virgin Mary is a most excellent Queen toward her people".

---

[86] St Bonaventure, *Sermon on the Royal Dignity of the Blessed Virgin Mary.*

SUSANNA: NON ESSET INVENTA IN EA RES TURPIS

Daniel said... 'You also have lied against your own head, for the angel of God is waiting with his sword to saw you in two, that he may destroy you both.' Then all the assembly shouted loudly and blessed God, who saves those who hope in him... And Hilkiah and his wife praised God for their daughter Susanna, and so did Joakim her husband and all her kindred, because nothing shameful was found in her.

— Dan 13:59-63 (RSVCE)

As Mordecai and Esther collaborated in saving their people, as the complementary actions of Barak and Jael won peace in their day, as Jephthah and his daughter offered one agonising sacrifice, as Joab cooperated with the wise woman of Abel to overcome an 'antichrist', so all these pairs point to Jesus and Mary redeeming and co-redeeming us from the Fall once brought about by Adam and Eve. We turn now to another man and woman, Daniel and Susanna, who were one in the work of God, again with markedly different tasks to discharge in securing relief for their community.[87]

The narrative, encapsulating the entire course of history, begins in a paradise (παράδεισος, *garden* Dan 13:4), involves murderous lies from the powerful, tends to an apocalypse

---

[87] Like the Book of Judith and key passages about Esther, the account of Susanna (Dan 13) does not appear in the Hebrew or Protestant Bibles, but is included in the Septuagint and Vulgate. Thereby it is given as an actual grace to Catholics and Orthodox for their guidance.

(ἀποκαλυφθῆναι, *unveiling* Dan 13:32) and ends with comprehensive judgement: condemnation of the wicked, deliverance of the innocent, and praise of God by the assembly of the just.

Susanna *"was exceedingly refined and beautiful in appearance"* (Dan 13:31). Two judges of Israel, stealing constant glances at her, become so inflamed with lust that they *"perverted their reason... so that they would not look to heaven, nor call to mind just judgments"* (Dan 13:9). They devise a scheme. Sliding silently through the garden, they wait until Susanna is alone, naked as Eve (for she was bathing), then demand she lie with them, threatening, if she refuses, to frame her with adultery. They are practised sexual predators.

> *You offspring of Canaan, and not of Judah, beauty has deceived you, and desire has perverted your heart. Thus did you do to the daughters of Israel, and they, out of fear, consorted with you, but a daughter of Judah would not tolerate your iniquity.* (Dan 13:56-57)

How many victims had they consumed, how many had they broken? If Susanna surrendered she would have been another unknown casualty and the predation would continue. If she resisted, the voracious judges would have her executed.

> *Susanna sighed, and said: I am straitened on every side: for if I do this thing, it is death to me: and if I do it not, I shall not escape your hands. But it is better for me to fall into your hands without doing it, than to sin in the sight of the Lord.* (Dan 13:22-23 DRB)

Susanna did not reckon submission to be sinless so long as she had a chance to resist. And she preferred to fall through death into God's hands than through choice to fall in with the corrupt judges. By her decision, although unknown to her, she was about to bring the insidious terror to an end.

Such is the exercise of a supremely free will. Immediately Susanna knew what was best to do; straight away she resolved to do it; and not for a moment did she falter as the dire consequences unfolded. The crosses which bear most fruit are not those for which in zeal we hunt, but those which God sends to us and which otherwise we never would choose. Freely embracing the predestined cross, as did Jesus and Mary, demonstrates unlimited love.

We see a like love in Susanna, who wore the cross of Christ. To be calumniated is a blow to the soul. To suffer disgrace in the eyes of family, servants and the public is a hammering.[88] You think a friend will stand by you but see in his unwonted silence or his uneasy withdrawal that good faith is gone. *"Friend and neighbour thou hast put far from me: and my acquaintance, because of misery"* (Ps 87:19 DRB). To be unjustly sentenced — as Susanna was to death — crushes

---

[88] Most of us taste some measure of this in life. As children, the light whipping of name-calling makes us smart unbearably; as teenagers the slightest betrayal is an outrage; as adults the experience of injustice shakes us to the core as we realise our powerlessness. If God, knowing our weakness, spares us, we are given instead to encounter suffering in others, for perchance this will wake us up to Jesus' suffering. In our cities we encounter men crushed by homelessness. In more places than we care to look souls are crushed by years of unpaid labour. In North Korea a whole population is crushed by totalitarianism. Today in the west, we feel crushed by the relentless march of modernism. All this being crushed has as its ultimate source the devil, so it is fitting, and will be a great relief, when the Woman crushes his head.

the spirit. One thinks evil might limit itself, might choose to desist. But the firmament seems to give way as you realise it never will. Only God puts limits on evil.

Susanna spent the night expecting to die on the coming day. She foresaw no escape but was certain she should not submit to the tyrants. Sometimes, when we do not know what to do, it is enough that we know what not to do, enduring in patience (Lk 21:19).

Day came, and having been summarily condemned in court, when Susanna was being *"led away to death, the Lord raised up the holy spirit"* (Dan 13:45) in young Daniel. *"Return to the place of judgment"* (Dan 13:49 RSVCE), he declares, and forcefully condemns the deceit of the murderous liars: *"You deep-rooted ancient evil, now your sins have come out, which you have committed before"* (Dan 13:52). Cross-examined, the two deviants inadvertently condemn themselves by their own mouths. Daniel declares:

> *Truly, you have lied against your own head. For behold, the angel of God, having received the sentence from him, will split you down the middle.* (Dan 13:55)[89]

As Jesus definitively stated those who sought to kill Him were not true sons of Abraham, not sons of God, but had the devil for their father (Jn 8:39-44), so Daniel states the wicked judges are not seed of Judah but of cursed Canaan, distinguishing the flesh from the spirit: *"You offspring of*

---

[89] The punishment is a wordplay on the type of tree the two defamers lied about. The point is that the words they said contain the method of their condemnation, as evil always entraps itself. Moreover, they too are lying like satan about the Tree.

Canaan, and not of Judah, beauty has deceived you, and desire has perverted your heart" (Dan 13:56). The devil had been ravished by his own radiance, a suicidal self-infatuation (Ezek 28:17).[90] Here in Babylon (Dan 13:1), the sin was preferring the allure of mortal flesh to the excelling purity of Susanna's spirit, esteeming matter before form.

For due punishment, some Greek textual variants relate that the assembly

> *did to them as they had done against their sister. Muzzling them, they brought them out, and cast them into a ravine: then the angel of the Lord poured fire through their midst* (Dan 13:62).

What vivid justice. The perpetrators experience *"fire through their midst"* — that is, the physical, psychological and spiritual hell they had first inflicted on their victims.

The Law insisted:

> *By the mouth of two or three witnesses, he who is to be put to death shall perish. Let no one be killed with only one person speaking testimony against him.* (Dt 17:6; cf. Heb 10:28)

The wisdom in this is not to suppose that one murderous liar cannot find a second or third to collaborate with him, but that if they do a wise judge will be able to expose where their testimonies conflict. The truth alone is integral, while falsity is

---

[90] St Thomas, *II Sent.* d.V q.1 a.3, "the first sin of the angel was pride… [F]rom the side of the desire, for he craved the eminence of dignity, but also on the part of the motive, for out of the consideration of his own beauty he fell into sin."

necessarily incoherent.[91] Hence the accusers of Jesus could not find agreement (Mk 14:56) and the accusers of Susanna were found out. The pair represent the forked tongue of the serpent, who slithered through the garden to tempt Eve when she was alone. Daniel interrogated them, asking *"under which tree"* the alleged infidelity took place. But the accusers contradicted each other. They who shamelessly insisted on the unveiling of the lady (Dan 13:32) were themselves exposed.[92]

Unveiled, prefiguring Mary, Susanna was

> *a very beautiful woman and one who feared the Lord. Her parents were righteous, and had taught their daughter according to the law of Moses.* (Dan 13:2-3 RSVCE)

She followed the Law, crying with a loud voice when under assault (Dt 22:24). When the assembly foolishly followed their corrupt leaders in condemning the innocent Susanna to death, she ardently prayed.[93]

---

[91] Jesus says: *"Even though I offer testimony about Myself, My testimony is true"* (Jn 8:14; cf. 5:30-32; 1 Jn 5:8). Everything Jesus says is one voice with the Father and Holy Ghost. The three testify as One, absolutely identically, discernible to the pure and the thoughtful in the ring of truth.

[92] Adam might have drilled into the deceit through which the serpent ensnared Eve (Gen 3:5) by asking: "Of which tree in the garden are you speaking?" Or "How can we avoid death, if God said by eating from or touching the tree we will die?" Or "How is it to be like gods, to know evil?" But such interrogation was saved for the day of Daniel and Susanna, or rather Jesus and Mary.

[93] *"The assembly believed them, because they were elders of the people and judges; and they condemned her to death"* (Dan 13:41). We are as guilty as these and the crowds who called for Jesus' death if we follow the evil of our ecclesial leaders: *"all things whatsoever that they shall say to you, observe and do. Yet truly, do not choose to act according to their works. For they say, but they do not do"* (Mt 23:3).

Susanna cried out with a loud voice and said, 'Eternal God, who knows what is hidden, who knows all things before they happen, you know that they have borne false witness against me, and behold, I must die, though I have done none of these things, which these men have maliciously invented against me.' But the Lord heeded her voice. (Dan 13:42-44)

Susanna's accomplishment was an absolute refusal to cooperate with evil. If one has literally no chance to escape, and no chance to defend oneself, and no chance to attack, God knows it. In such cases, prayer and the refusal to consent to evil are enough. Deliverance, whether in time or eternity, is in God's Hands.

Meanwhile, so evident was Susanna's chastity, that just to hear it questioned hurt pious ears:

after the old men had spoken, the servants were greatly ashamed, for there had never been anything of this kind said about Susanna. (Dan 13:27)

Correspondingly, the Church has always defended, against enemies who insinuate otherwise, the perpetual virginity of the Blessed Virgin Mary, by which heresies are destroyed.[94]

Susanna's vindication caused joy among all her people:

---

[94] Tract for Marian Feasts after Septuagesima: "Rejoice, O Virgin Mary; alone you have put an end to all heresies. You who believed the words of the Archangel Gabriel. Still a virgin, you brought forth God and man; and after childbirth you remained an inviolate virgin."

And Hilkiah and his wife praised God for their daughter Susanna, and so did Joakim her husband and all her kindred, because nothing shameful was found in her [non esset inventa in ea res turpis]. (Dan 13:63 RSVCE)

So the Catholic Church sings: "Thou art all fair, O Mary, there is no spot of original sin in thee."[95] Strength is not only driving pegs through a man's skull or hurling millstones to crush a head or slicing through a neck with a sword. Greater fortitude lies in resisting sin, even at the risk of one's life. That is spiritual power. Susanna's chastity was a force which hurt no one, but those who assailed it found themselves crushed. Likewise whoever refuses to repent piercing with thorns the Immaculate Heart of Mary.

Our Lady's triumph is not only eschatological in the final defeat of satan. It is in every generation, in every soul who calls on her aid. In her *Fiat* Mary undid satan's corruption of Eve; on Calvary, by imitating Her divine Son perfectly, she broke the devil's reign of terror over human creatures. In each generation Mary assists souls to participate in degrees of chastity according to their state: consecrated virgins, celibate priests, married couples who in purity of mind embrace bodily for the sake of increasing life, and the unmarried. In these various states evil is overcome.

---

[95] On the Feast of the Immaculate Conception, at Mass and Vespers the Church prays: *"Tota pulchra es, María, et macula originalis non est in te."* cf. *"You are totally beautiful, my love, and there is no blemish in you"* (Cant 4:7). At Mass the Tract continues: "Happy are you, O holy Virgin Mary, and most worthy of all praise, who with your virgin foot have crushed the serpent's head."

All of us are called to imitate Susanna as she imitates Mary. Susanna refused to sin, even though she could not save herself from the wrath of the corrupt judges. Daniel could save her, and did so, having regard for her innocence. Likewise Jesus will save those souls who, being awarded innocence by baptism, seek to maintain it by confession.

Moreover, it was by Susanna's defiance of temptation (*bzw.* threats) that the judges were exposed and condemned, to the benefit of all. Had Susanna surrendered, then the whole people would have continued to be at risk from these perfidious predators. In a related way, Our Lady is Co-Redemptrix. She did not save herself, for it is still by the Cross that her Redemption is won, albeit pre-emptively in her unique conception. But because Mary is sinless and waits on Christ, the enemy is defeated (including corrupt cardinals). This bringing down of the mighty by the innocent waiting on God, the lowly being elevated, is at the centre of her Magnificat. Jesus too assures us of it: *"Blessed are you who are weeping now, for you shall laugh"* (Lk 6:21). Susanna and Daniel show us on a local level what Jesus and Mary achieved universally.

Postscript

Interestingly, in the Vulgate the very last line of this chapter, after due recognition is given to Susanna and to Daniel, suddenly speaks of a dramatic change in government.

> *there had been found in [Susanna] no disgrace. And so Daniel became great in the sight of the people from that*

120

day, and thereafter. And king Astyages was laid to rest with his fathers. And Cyrus the Persian received his kingdom. (Dan 13:63-65)

This arrangement carries a profound meaning. If we take Susanna to prefigure the Virgin Mary, and we read here of her successfully bearing her hardest trial, which can only mean Calvary; and if Daniel prefigures Jesus, here we read of him becoming *"great in the sight of the people from that day, and thereafter"*, which again is perfectly appropriate to point to the Paschal Mystery; what was the consequence at the highest level of government, representing the Heavens? King Astyages dies and Emperor Cyrus ascends to the throne. There is much more to this than meets the eye.

Astyages, King of the Medes, was a wretched tyrant who, according to the historian Herodotus, ordered the death of his own grandson after having a bad dream. Discovering ten years later that the sentence had not been carried out, he had the responsible courtier's son boiled and roasted and tricked the murdered boy's father at a banquet into eating him.[96] The account is so gruesome that many write it off as a myth. The truth is worse, with satan tricking today's generation into devouring their children through commodifying embryos.

Thankfully, Astyages was the last king in his line, being dethroned by Emperor Cyrus the Great. Cyrus overthrew three empires to establish the vast and tolerant Achaemenid Empire. Most significantly, in his first year as King of Kings, inspired

---

[96] Herodotus, *Histories*, I, 119.

by God, he ended the Babylonian exile of the Jews, decreeing that they should go up to Jerusalem and rebuild the House of the Lord, the Temple (2 Chron 36:22-23; Ezra 1:1-4), which was indeed accomplished.

This history, condensed to two short sentences, has entered the Bible for a reason higher than its literal meaning. The whole of Daniel 13 relates the trial of Susanna and her salvation by Daniel, until this last line in the Vulgate suddenly speaks of the deposing of a cruel tyrant, overthrown by the King of Kings, who in turn establishes peace and orders the erection of God's House. Is that not a picture of the result of the Paschal Mystery of Our Lord? That the devil fell like lightning from the sky and Jesus, the King of Kings, ascended to be enthroned at the Right Hand of the Father, there to oversee the commencement of the building of the Church, stone by stone, word by word, soul by soul.

This is a suitable summary coming at the end of our seventh prefiguration of a woman, in combination with a man, crushing the enemy's head. There is praise of the woman, meaning Mary. There is praise of the man, meaning Jesus. There is the death of the tyrant, meaning satan. And there is the enthronement of a divinely inspired king, the Son of God. It is all there, in the Vulgate's final three verses of Daniel 13.

II: Mary Pondered All These Words in Her Heart

G od writes His Plan into the Scriptures confident that those who have faith will find it, and be guided by it. His enemies are often too proud to read the Scriptures, or those who do are too faithless to understand what they read. If we want to know God, and if we wish our spirit to survive the trials of this life and the Last Day, then humble and prayerful persistence in reading the Bible will guide us. It is not meant to be easy, but it is always rewarding. If we love God, we will make the effort.

How much did Jesus understand of His mission, by meditating upon the Law, Prophets and Psalms? Everything essential. How much did Mary understand of her unique vocation by pondering the Word of God? More than we imagine. How much of our own calling can we understand by attentively reading Sacred Scripture?[97] Much, for it is given to us with reason. Let us take Mary for our example.

After the Annunciation, Mary would have certainly re-read the Scriptures with an attentiveness greater than when she was a girl. Mary knew from the message of the angel that the Son she conceived was the Messiah. Our Lady *"kept all these words, pondering them in her heart"* (Lk 2:19). With new eyes Mary read Genesis, God's words to the serpent:

> *I will put enmities between you and the woman, between your offspring and her offspring. She will crush your head, and you will lie in wait for her heel.* (Gen 3:15)

Mary knew her Jesus was the *"offspring"* promised from the beginning and therefore she was *"the woman"*. How resolute she must have been never to act as Eve did to Adam, never to draw the New Adam away from God's command. Much more she sought to be *"a helper similar to"* Him (Gen 2:20,18).

At some point Our Lady realised, before any other human, that the Messiah was greater than all had expected: True Man and True God. Mary would consider especially all that was said in the Tanakh of God's Anointed, God's Suffering Servant, including Crucifixion and Resurrection. And though

---

[97] Sacred art, with profound theological accuracy, loves to depict St Anne teaching her daughter Mary to read the Scriptures, as also the Mother of God reading the same with her divine Son. This family did not rely on their ontological excellence to know the truth simply by infusion, but in wisdom worked at it too, reading and pondering the scrolls. So we, by contemplating the insights of the Fathers and heeding the Magisterium, can go to the Bible daily to hear from God.

not everything was immediately open when the rediscovered Word of God said, *"did you not know that it is necessary for Me to be in these things which are of My Father?"*, once again *"His mother kept all these words in her heart"* (Lk 2:49,51).

How often did Mary revisit the verse where Eve

gave birth to a son, and she called his name Seth, saying, 'God has given me another offspring, in place of Abel, whom Cain killed'. (Gen 4:25)

Did Mary see here that God's Plan could not be stopped by death? Did her heart blaze when she read some twenty times in בראשית the worldwide blessing God would give through the *"offspring"* (Gen 3:15; 9:9; 12:7; 13:15-16; 15:5,18; 16:10; 17:7-10,19; 21:12-13,17-18; 24:7; 26:3-4,24; 28:4,13-14; 32:12; 35:12; 48:4,19)? Yet also the terrible cost, requiring readiness to sacrifice the only-begotten:

By my own self, I have sworn, says the Lord. Because you have done this thing, and have not spared your only begotten son for my sake, I will bless you, and I will multiply your offspring like the stars of heaven, and like the sand which is on the seashore. Your offspring will possess the gates of their enemies. And in your offspring, all the nations of the earth will be blessed, because you obeyed my voice. (Gen 22:16-18)

When Mary read Judges and saw Jael piercing evil Sisera's skull with a peg, presumably she recalled God's Word to the devil: *"She will crush your head."* And Mary saw Jael walked secretly, mysteriously, that Jael's demeanour was kind and recollected, though fully focused on her opportunity to defend God's People from their cruel enemy.

What more did Our Lady learn from the woman from Thebez, who cast a millstone on Abimelech's head? The wicked aggressor repeated his battle plan; that which succeeded against Shechem he sought to replay in Thebez. Did Mary consider the former attacks on the prophets, and see the same might be done to her Son? Mary knew the prophets were not defeated by death. Forever after they were held in esteem and their words continued to save Israel. So the Mother of God did not fear the death of her Son would be the end of His work.

Jephthah's daughter whispered to Mary the call to total self-sacrifice. Loving God above one's life would hurt. Did Mary have a special love for Jephthah's daughter: the only person in the entire OT who for the sake of God's Word willingly gave her life in a holocaust when she could conceivably have just walked away?

With the wise woman of Abel, Mary knew that evil divides — all the forces of Judah against Israel in one vulnerable city: why have them slaughter each other in battle when all they have to do is reject the son of Bichri, reject sin, and say 'no' to his summons? Then he is finished and the people have peace.

Mary saw Judith succeeded, and Esther interceded with the King, and Susanna too was ready to die rather than cooperate with evil, relying on God and on His servant for her defence, not on the elders and rulers of Israel. Contemplating these key facts braced Mary for her long approach to Calvary.

Mary's preparation was long indeed. Jael's action had been spontaneous, taking a few minutes, albeit from a strength of character built by a lifetime of seeking God. With the woman of Thebez, the battle surged for some hours. The woman of Abel bore her burden probably for some days or weeks, less time than it takes to build ramparts. Judith did her work in half a week. Esther endured for much longer, about two months until the murderous decree was superseded. Susanna's trial lasted two days, from horror to exoneration and rejoicing. But Jephthah's daughter carried her burden for two months, a decree which was not superseded. She did not waver. Her will was totally free. Of all these women she was the one who paid with her life, though the others had all risked theirs.

Jephthah's daughter wielded no hammer, heaved no rock in the heat of battle, sought no strategy to escape from disaster, hacked at nobody's neck with a sword, called for no one to be hung on a gibbet, and did not even protest her innocence. How purely spiritual was this girl's combat, how sweet her soul's self-surrender. What an agony it caused for her father. The virgin's thoughts were to console him. What a triumph of grace, her selflessness under duress! The greatest fight to be had is not physical, the ultimate war is not going to be nuclear, but in the spirit God gains His victory, in the soul which refuses to sin, in the heart which never ceases to trust. It is on this all history turns.

If we can find Marian prefigurations in the Scriptures, it is likely that, among all creatures, Our Lady found them first.

Her conversations with Jesus about the meaning of the Scriptures, we can scarcely imagine.

When the day came, on Calvary, Mary knew her Son Jesus would crush satan. Regardless of whether her Torah read *"he will crush"* or *"she will crush"*, Mary wanted to be a helpmate to her Adam. She sought not to protest poor Pilate, nor curse corrupt Caiaphas and Annas. She hated not one of the soldiers who whipped off the skin of her Child, nor resented the bloodlust of her people when they cried *"Crucify!"*; crucify an innocent Man. Mary did not strike at the infantile elders, nor cast a stone at the murderous pharisees, nor spit on the sin-sunken Sadducees, nor argue with the illegal court. There were among these true enemies of God, but Our Lady was not there to break a bruised reed nor quench a smouldering wick. *Aquila non capit muscas*. Mother Mary by offering her dearest Son to the Father; by wavering not once against His Will; by trusting her Jesus was stronger than death; by not falling into sin during this heaviest trial: Our Lady crushed satan's head. Here was a soul satan could not accuse. Here was one who would not only avoid hell, but also who would not be contained by death. Mary would be assumed body and soul straight to Heaven when she died.

With the united sacrifice of Jesus and Mary on Calvary, satan's winning streak was over. In fact it was exposed as an illusion. It had never been a winning streak, but all had been in God's service for the greater glorification of those who love Him. First His Son, second Mary, then the rest. For satan, this is a total crushing.

III: FOUR WOMEN ANNOUNCE THE ANNUNCIATION

There are details written into the opening lines of the New Testament which are easy to overlook, but if they are considered carefully and placed in the context we have been studying so far, do yield an immense return. St Matthew helps us discover how the Annunciation was announced, multiple times, long before it actually happened. It is as if everything were engineered to ensure it.

I might be wrong in the sections which follow (as also in those which precede). But I am exploring a seam in Scripture which has been mined for thousands of years and still seems inexhaustible. It has more gold to give. Prefigurations, like dogmas, can take millennia to come into focus.

Our Lady's defeat of the Antichrist is realised in various stages. The first was passive, Mary's Immaculate Conception, where by a singular privilege her body and soul were preserved from all stain of sin. After this came Mary's *Fiat* at the Annunciation, when she unconditionally accepted God's Will for her, the devil still having no part in her. Most decisive was Mary's will on Calvary, actively offering her Son to the Father. Theoretically, this was the devil's best chance to induce Jesus' Mother to sin, yet he lost utterly and never recovered. Mary's Dormition sealed her perfect life.

Following all this, through history singular saints have been inspired and assisted by the Virgin Mary to achieve great holiness, overcoming momentous evil: St Bernard the first Cistercian; St Clara of Assisi first abbess of the Poor Clares; St Catherine of Siena a Dominican tertiary; St Louis Marie de Montfort founder of the Company of Mary; St Alphonsus Ligouri a Redemptorist, patron of confessors and moral theologians; St Maximilian Kolbe a Franciscan; St Teresa of Calcutta foundress of the Missionaries of Charity. All these assisted in bringing certain other souls with theirs to Heaven. In their "limited" ways, these saints show how the "unlimited" greatness of the Mediatrix of all Graces is fruitful in the lives of, literally, all God's children. Thereby Mary deprives satan of his prey. Another victory for Our Lady.

Finally, the most dramatic triumph for Mary's Immaculate Heart is reserved for the end of time. All those souls who are devoted to the Virgin Mary will, by her assistance, overcome in history the entire plan of the last and most terrible

Antichrist. So God will put an absolute end to the struggle between good and evil which has raged since the first generation (Apoc 20:9-10).

The connection between all these phases lies in the constancy of Mary's will, entirely devoted to God: *"Behold, I am the handmaid of the Lord. Let it be done to me according to your word"* (Lk 1:38; cf. Mt 6:10; Lk 22:42; Jn 6:38). This famous *Fiat* of Our Lady complements the Incarnation. When the human received the divine, the divine assumed the human. As the Passion of Christ is prefigured many times, so also, given its indispensability, is the Incarnation, which was immediately effected upon Mary's *Fiat* at the Annunciation.

So central to God's plan is this commerce that He prefigured the miraculous conception of Jesus seven times in the OT, making the eighth to be Mary's, as eight represents completion, surplus or a new beginning. The prefigurations involved Sarah, Rebekah, Rachel, the unnamed mother of Samson, Hannah mother of Samuel, the Shunammite woman and, in prophecy, Sion.[98] All these cooperated with God: *"Who maketh a barren woman to dwell in a house, the joyful mother of children"* (Ps 112:9 DRB).

As mentioned, the perfection of Mary's *Fiat* is intrinsically linked to her offering her all on Calvary, her victory over satan. Both these are linked also with her triumph at the end of time, as foretold in Eden when God sentenced satan, saying:

---

[98] Gen 11:30; 25:21; 30:22; Jdg 13:3; 1 Sam 1:5; 2 Kngs 4:16; Is 49:21; 54:1. If the seventh example is too figurative then, before the New Covenant was inaugurated, there is also St Elizabeth who was barren, yet by a miraculous intervention, like the other six women listed, conceived a son (Lk 1:7,36).

"She will crush your head" (Gen 3:15). We have studied seven other women who crushed the serpent's head in prefiguration, making Mary again the eighth. These were Jael, the woman of Thebez, Jephthah's Daughter, the wise woman of Abel, Judith, Esther and Susanna.[99]

To help us recognise the connection between these two great events — Our Lady conceiving and Our Lady triumphing — there are in the OT a further four women, each of whom foreshadows both events: the beginning and the end, the promise and the triumph, the seed and its fruit. They are Tamar, Rahab, Ruth and Bathsheba. It is highly significant that they are the only women named with Mary by St Matthew as he establishes Jesus' genealogy (Mt 1:1-17).

This genealogy points to Jesus through Mary by first listing a long line of generations from Abraham to St Joseph, then Joseph's marriage to Mary and finally, through her, the birth of Jesus. Of all the men listed, two are given special mention with Jesus in the very first verse of the Gospels: David and Abraham.[100] They are selected, explains St Jerome, to remind us Jesus' Advent was promised long beforehand by God, the Messiah a descendant of Abraham and David in the flesh.[101]

---

[99] Jdg 4:21; Jdg 9:53; Jdg 11:36; 2 Sam 20:22; Jud 13:10; Est 11:2-10; Dan 13:44.

[100] We may see a gentle portrayal of the Blessed Trinity here: *"The book of the lineage of Jesus Christ, the son of David, the son of Abraham"* (Mt 1:1). Jesus is the Son; David the man of the Spirit; Abraham the figure of the Father. So the NT shows the Holy Trinity stands at the beginning of everything, of all generations.

[101] See St Jerome, *Commentary on St Matthew's Gospel*, I, for this observation on God's promises to Abraham (Gen 22:18 DRB) and David (Ps 88:4; 131:11 DRB).

As no word is wasted in the Bible, what might the meaning be of the four women who are mentioned in the genealogy? Might they help us understand the role of Mary? Their personal histories were spread over several centuries and at first glance appear unrelated. It is only through St Matthew's including them in Jesus' genealogy that the thought occurs to compare them to each other.

Certain Church Fathers explained that the four women are mentioned to demonstrate that Jesus took His Flesh not only from a Hebrew lineage. He descended also from Gentiles thereby indicating His Mission to save not Jews alone, but Gentiles too. The saying is true, but it is questionable whether this was St Matthew's full reason. Though Rahab was a Canaanite and Ruth a Moabitess, it is possible Tamar, and more likely Bathsheba, were born Hebrews.[102]

An alternative explanation offered by the Fathers is that the four women show that Jesus came to associate with sinners and to overcome sin, and therefore He was not ashamed to have in His biological ancestry the duplicitous Tamar, the prostitute Rahab, a contemptible Moabitess and the adulterous Bathsheba. Again the saying is true, but nor can this be the full explanation. Tamar is excused of sin by her circumstances; Rahab is a heroine; Ruth is presented by the Scriptures as a

---

[102] Though Judah took a Canaanite woman as his wife (Gen 38:2), Jewish commentaries say Tamar, who was chosen to wed their son Er, was an Israelite, though in their day there cannot have been many Israelites from which to choose. And while Bathsheba was married to a Hittite, Uriah, some point out that she must be Hebrew if the Eliam named as her father (2 Sam 11:3) is the same as the Hebrew Eliam son of Ahitopel, one of the thirty (2 Sam 23:34).

paragon of virtue; Bathsheba's guilt does not compare to David's. On that note, enough of Jesus' male ancestors were evident sinners that there was no need to add these women to the list just to underline His sweet tolerance of us.

The key to understanding their presence lies in the fifth woman mentioned in the list, Mary of Nazareth. St Matthew had listed lots of forefathers of Jesus but right at the end, instead of repeating once again the formula of fatherhood, he switches the focus: *"...and Jacob the father of Joseph the husband of Mary, of whom Jesus was born, who is called Christ"* (Mt 1:16). St Joseph was truly the husband of Mary but only the *"supposed"* father of Jesus, as St Luke explicitly writes (Lk 3:23; cf. Mt 13:55; Mk 6:3; Jn 6:42). This is the link between the five women. For if anyone were to doubt that God is the true Father of Jesus, they may study the cases of the four women mentioned earlier in the genealogy, and will observe that each one of them conceived by someone greater than their supposed husband. This run of surprises is a multi-millennial preparation for the biggest surprise of all: a virgin conceiving by the power of God the Holy Ghost.

That the four OT women have in common conceiving by someone greater than their supposed husband might be nothing more than a curiosity. However, given the Scriptures show us no other women in Jesus' ancestry to whom this criterion applies, combined with the fact that no other women are mentioned in St Matthew's genealogy, suggests this was the reason he listed them. If this is the intended link between them, then in Mary's case we may ask: who can possibly be greater than St Joseph, a just man, of the tribe of Judah, the heir of the royal house and family of David, a perfect saint (Mt 1:19; Lk 1:27; 2:4)? Who is the greater one by whom Mary actually conceived? The only suitable answer is God.

It was never in St Matthew's power to invent the stories of Tamar, Rahab, Ruth and Bathsheba. It could not have occurred to any chronicler in the days of these women to falsify the record in the knowledge of whereto their stories were leading. Only God can arrange these things, preserve them forever in the public space, then inspire His chosen evangelist to link them together. There is a saying: "Once is happenstance; twice is coincidence; three times is enemy action." As this is clearly not the work of the enemy, then we can happily conclude that "four times" reveals the Hand of God. The only possible sufficient cause for this exalted harmony is His Wisdom and Providence. These four women announce the Annunciation some 1,000 to 1,700 years before it happened and, by their virtues, they foreshadow Mary's defeat of the Antichrist. There might be a better explanation as to why the four appear in the genealogy, but any lesser explanation seems fragmentary.

Some might find this scandalous: shall an incestuous deceiver, a traitorous prostitute, a gold-digging seducer and an adulterous exhibitionist be figures for the Immaculate Mother of God? But Sacred Scripture has its own rules. If a lion can represent Jesus or satan; if fire can represent Heaven or hell; if water can represent life or death; if a rock can signify our foundation or our doom; then there is no problem if imperfect persons stand as types for the Mother of God.

To take scandal here is to forget that Jesus came to redeem sinners. It is to overlook the stark fact that all these women were biological ancestors of God made Man.[103] And it is to misread their individual situations, where sin is sometimes wrongly imputed. There is much to admire in each of the four women. And if we recognise how decisive their actions were for the fulfilment of God's plan in the course of salvation history, then we may even be awed by them.

Finally, whatever St Matthew's actual reasons were for including the four women before mentioning Mary, the search here is more concerned with God's reasons. He is the ultimate author of the Scriptures, and He wishes to communicate truths to us of which even His instrumental authors were not always aware at the time of writing. That said, as there is every reason to suppose St Matthew spent time conversing with Our Lady, then it could easily be that she sowed seeds in his mind, meaning it is perfectly possible that God's reasons and Our Lady's reasons and St Matthew's reasons all coincide. It is worth searching!

---

[103] Our Lady was of the House of David, meaning she had Tamar, Rahab and Ruth in her ancestry. And if as tradition supposes, St Matthew and St Luke give the ancestries of St Joseph and Mary respectively, then Bathsheba figures in both, as mother of Solomon (Mt 1:6) and as mother of Nathan (Lk 3:31). So Bathsheba too is in the ancestry of Mary. In any case St Joseph and Mary were related by blood. See St John Damascene, *An Exposition of the Orthodox Faith*, IV, 14 (on the Feast of St Joachim, Father of the Blessed Virgin Mary, Matins, *Lectiones* VII-IX).

Tamar: More Just than Judah

The theme of a woman conceiving by someone greater than her supposed husband is absolutely unambiguous in Tamar's case. She became pregnant not by her first husband, Er, who *"was wicked in the sight of the Lord; and the Lord slew him"* (Gen 38:7 RSVCE). She became pregnant not by her second husband, Onan, the prototype of contraception, who *"spilled [his] semen on the ground... And what he did was displeasing in the sight of the Lord, and he slew him also"* (Gen 38:9-10 RSVCE). Nor did Tamar become pregnant by the least of the husbands owed to her, Shelah, younger brother of the first two (Gen 38:1-26). Instead she conceived by one greater than all of these, namely their father, Judah, most blessed of Israel's twelve patriarchs.

The whole thing was such a well-kept secret that, until there was a dramatic revelation, literally nobody but Tamar knew who the father of her child was, not even Judah. In this we have a foreshadowing of the Blessed Virgin Mary, who alone among humans knew how she had become pregnant, until the mystery was revealed to others.

St Augustine defends Tamar who, in extreme circumstances, exerted herself to have children.[104] It is fully in accord with natural law for a woman to yearn to give life. It accords with divine law too: the first command God gave was to *"increase and multiply"* (Gen 1:28). Tamar was not a close relative of Judah, and she was unmarried when she disguised

---

[104] St Augustine, *Contra Faustum*, XII, 64.

herself as a prostitute and he went into her. That we should not condemn Tamar, on legal or moral grounds, is substantiated by verdict of Judah who admitted *"she is more just than I am"* (Gen 38:26).

It was Judah's duty, and he promised, to give her in marriage to his third son Shelah. But as his first two sons had died, he was afraid, and hesitated, and delayed. And Tamar saw the years passing away, her marital rights being unjustly obstructed. Had she not acted as she did, how else should the promised Messiah come into the world? Judah had failed in his duty, had turned deaf to his calling to maintain the law. Subsequently he admitted it. Tamar rescued the situation, without which St Matthew's genealogy would have expired in the fifth generation rather than reaching its proper end.

The final triumph of Our Lady is intimated in the switch from looming death to blessed life. At first, Judah did not acknowledge his own offspring. On learning Tamar was pregnant, and suspecting fornication, Judah condemned mother and child to be executed, saying, *"Bring her out, and let her be burned"* (Gen 38:24). But thanks be to God, and to Tamar's foresight, she had secured three signs from him of his paternity so that, when after her condemnation she produced them for him to see, he realised he was the father, confessed his fault and looked after mother and child. In fact, children, for Tamar was pregnant with twins.

Is not this honest act by Judah precisely what the Jews are called to do? They do not realise that Judaism is the true father of Christianity. They imagine Christianity is foreign, unclean.

Indeed, in the early centuries, there were Jews who would gladly have seen the Church and her children executed. But once the Jews see that the Church is in possession of the pledges of continuity — Judah's signet ring, cord and staff (Gen 38:18,25) — will they not be moved as he was to reconciliation? Specifically, if the Jews examine the Church's rites and heritage, will they not, with hearts unveiled, recognise them as their own heritage? For the Holy Sacrifice of the Mass fulfils the sacrifices offered by Abraham, and the activities in Moses' Tent of Meeting, and likewise the rites of Solomon's Temple. For a catalyst, once the Jews grow aware of the pious affection and liturgical honours with which Catholics esteem the Patriarchs and Prophets, might hostility not turn to fraternal affection? It is something to pray for most solemnly. Perhaps Tamar points to this succeeding.

Judah lost the marks of election, and was too embarrassed to ask around for them, not wanting to admit his worldly, carnal diversion with a prostitute. But Tamar, like the Church, treasured them for the sake of her children's lives, and her own life and for Judah's success too. She did not just take their offspring and run, but wanted her son Perez to inherit Judah's blessing and that Judah would not die without knowing his offspring. Tamar risked her life to achieve all this. She signifies Catholicism; Judah signifies Judaism; and Perez signifies Jesus Christ.

First Tamar considered the situation, then she planned carefully the time and the place, and, understanding in advance the dangers involved, she secured precisely those items which would save the day, namely Judah's signet ring, cord and staff. What might these three mean?

It is no coincidence that the items are linked with the High Priest yet to come, the spiritual head of all God's People, Jesus Christ. They are pledges because it all happened long before this High Priest, or even Aaron, was even born.

Firstly, the signet ring is used for imprinting a seal, to communicate both the identity of the owner and that his authority is vested in whomever bears the ring. This very same word, חוֹתָם (seal, signet), is used three times in describing the unique vestments of the High Priest (Ex 28:11,21,36).[105] If we accept this association between the identity which Judah communicated and that of Israel's High Priest, then God indicates that a second High Priest must come with a New Covenant, for the three links are repeated after the renewal of the Covenant (Ex 39:6,14,29).[106] So we are not ultimately thinking of Aaron or a High Priest of the tribe of Levi as promised by Judah, but of Jesus Christ, Eternal High Priest.

Secondly, the cord, פָּתִיל, which Judah lent to Tamar as a pledge, is also associated with the High Priest, for fixing the

---

[105] The onyx stones on the shoulder pieces with the names of the twelve tribes of Israel inscribed as a signet upon them; his breast-piece of twelve precious stones with the same names inscribed as a signet upon them; and for his crown, a golden plate fixed to his turban upon which was inscribed like a signet — קֹדֶשׁ לַיהוָה — "Holy to the Lord".

[106] That is, God had once written the Law on the two stone tablets which Moses then smashed on account of the idolatry and fornication before the Golden Calf. In the renewal of the Mosaic Covenant a second set of stone tablets had the Law written on them, and these would endure in the ark of the covenant, a sign that a New Covenant would come — carried in Our Lady.

breast-piece to the ephod with a *"cord of blue"*, of refined craftsmanship, and likewise for attaching the golden plate to his headdress (Ex 28:28,37). Again these associations are repeated after the Covenant is renewed (Ex 39:20,30). Now these *"cords of blue"* which adorn the High Priest were to be worn by every son of Israel in order that they *"remember all the commandments of the Lord"* (see Num 15:37-40).[107] Truly we may think of the High Priest Jesus vested in Mary, and all Christians imitating Him in being coloured by Mary too. This is so that we remember the commandment of the Lord, and be holy to Him, so that He may be our God. Jesus shows us that we are meant to achieve this by wearing Marian blue.

Finally, the third item given in pledge was Judah's מַטֶּה, his staff. More than half of the 250-plus times this word is used in the Bible, it means *"tribe"*, especially in association with the twelve tribes of Israel. It is used also to mean *"sceptre"*, a symbol of royal sovereignty, and elsewhere to mean *"branch"*. If these three meanings all tie in with the Crucifixion, or else simply because it is made of wood, then Judah's *"staff"* may stand for Jesus' Cross.[108]

---

[107] *"The Lord also said to Moses: 'Speak to the sons of Israel, and you shall tell them to make for themselves hems at the corners of their cloaks, placing in them ribbons of hyacinth [bzw. "cords of blue"], so that, when they see these, they may remember all the commandments of the Lord, and they may not follow their own thoughts and eyes, fornicating in various ways, but instead, they, being more mindful of the precepts of the Lord, may do them and may be holy to their God.'"*

[108] The twelve *"tribes"* are now those who, like the Apostles, take up their crosses to follow Christ. The Cross signifies royalty supreme, being the throne and *"sceptre"* of the King of Kings. We are *"branches"* of *"the true vine"* if we partake of the Blood which He poured out on the Cross.

These three signs of authority departed from Judah, but were carefully retained by Tamar, then returned to him. This signifies the Covenant beginning with the Jews, passing to the Church, then returning to the Jews as they join the Church, yet without ever departing from Jesus (cf. Gen 49:10).[109] The drama of salvation history spanning several millennia of history is condensed into a few lines relating the lives of Judah and Tamar:

Judah said, 'Produce her, so that she may be burned.' But when she was led out to the punishment, she sent to her father-in-law, saying: 'I conceived by the man to whom these things belong. Recognise whose ring, and bracelet, and staff this is.' But he, acknowledging the gifts, said: 'She is more just than I am.' (Gen 38:24-26)

Thus Tamar, once suspected, was exonerated. With words bearing tremendous significance for the far future, Tamar said: *"I conceived by the man to whom these belong."* Might Mary declare something similar in the end times to some of those who are hostile to the Church? Might she demonstrate to chosen souls, even to those *"as yet breathing out threatenings and slaughter against the disciples of the Lord"* (Acts 9:1),

---

[109] Tamar asks Judah to give her as a pledge his חוֹתָם , that is *"seal"* (Gen 38:18). The word occurs some fourteen times in the Bible, including twice in the Canticle describing Christ's marriage to the Church, and the Church's desire to belong to Him: *"Set me like a seal upon your heart, like a seal upon your arm"* (Cant 8:7). But when she returns it to Judah, she uses the word חֹתֶמֶת, *"signet ring"*, which is a *hapax legomenon* — it occurs only once in the entire Bible. There has been a change, a unique identity is being intimated, one sealed with His own seal, that is Jesus Christ anointed, sealed, by the Holy Ghost.

that in fact she was sealed by and conceived by the Holy Ghost, by God Himself, and so convert those like Saul who are at enmity with her children? If those Jews who are searching for their heritage — the Temple, the priesthood, the daily sacrifices — will examine what the Church presents to them, will they not recognise the heritage they once lost is in fact all there in Holy Mass and the Divine Office?[110]

In the space of a few months Tamar prefigured both the Annunciation and Our Lady's triumph. First, by quietly conceiving by someone greater than her supposed husband. And then, by arranging the recognition by Judah that the mother was without sin, and that the son is in fact his own, so that rather than have them killed, they live harmoniously as one family. This small seed, by the time of the eschaton, will be the greatest reconciliation ever. That will be a triumph worth all the pains of history. When in the end it all happens, it will happen quickly.

---

[110] Was it not God Himself Who designated through the Torah the signs of identity and continuity, and are these not somehow Trinitarian: the unique signet seal for the Holy Ghost; the cord of the Eternal High Priest the Son; and the staff that of the Law Giver, the Head of the People, the Father?

RAHAB: BE MINDFUL OF RAHAB

The Holy Spirit says in the Psalms: *"I will be mindful of Rahab... knowing me"* (Ps 86:4). We should be mindful of her, too, for in her mysteries are hidden.

We recall Tamar conceived by Judah, greater than her expected husband Shelah. In the case of Rahab, a prostitute of Jericho, she might have conceived by any number of incontinent Gentiles in the doomed city. Instead she married and conceived by Salmon, member of God's Chosen People, again of the tribe of Judah. One of the two spies, he was brave, capable and trusted. He was a prince, his father being the leader of Judah in the days of Moses (Num 1:4-7; Mt 1:4). In this sense she conceived by a greater person than one might otherwise have expected, thereby prefiguring Our Lady.[111]

By her virtues, Rahab played a decisive role in Israel's triumph over Jericho, a victory which was so singular, complete and divine that it signalled God was with Israel for their entering and inhabiting the whole Holy Land. Rahab was merciful, quick-thinking, courageous, prudent and, above all, she had faith in the true God. In Jericho, Rahab's household alone was saved, showing the necessity for all who wish to escape from this doomed world alive of cleaving to Mary the Mother of God.

---

[111] St James wrote that the reason for Rahab's justification was for *"receiving the messengers and sending them out through another way"* (Jas 2:25). He uses the word ἀγγέλους (angels) for the messengers. We may think of the Virgin Mary receiving the heavenly messenger, for at the close of their encounter Rahab gave her *Fiat: "Just as you have spoken, so let it be done"* (Josh 2:21 cf. *"...fiat mihi secundum verbum tuum. Et discessit ab illa angelus"* Lk 1:38).

It would be wrong-headed to discount Rahab as a traitor to her people, for there is nothing treacherous about abandoning opponents of God to side with His People. Thereby, like Mary, she saved her household. Nor should we be troubled that Rahab was a prostitute. Our Lord was pleased to choose a former prostitute to be His Apostle to the Apostles. Already having so pure a Mother, Jesus demonstrates by such choices that He is for all. For his part, St Paul has nothing but praise for Rahab, writing her into a shortlist of the OT elite on account of her faith. She is there with Abraham, Isaac, Jacob, Joseph, Moses, the whole people of Israel, and then, as the seventh: *"By faith, Rahab, the harlot, did not perish with the unbelievers, after receiving the spies with peace"* (Heb 11:31). It is by her faith that Rahab anticipates Mary the Mother of God, and it is in this light we contemplate her conceiving and her decisive actions in Israel's apocalyptic triumph.

The cause of Rahab's great faith was grace, enlightening her when she rightly considered the works of the Lord and consequently chose to assist the two spies:

I know that the Lord has given this land to you. For the terror of you has fallen upon us, and all the inhabitants of the land have languished. We have heard that the Lord dried up the water of the Red Sea upon your arrival, when you were departing from Egypt, and we heard of the things that you did to the two kings of the Amorites, who were beyond the Jordan, Sihon and Og, whom you put to death. And upon hearing these things, we were very afraid, and our heart languished. Neither

*did there remain in us any spirit at your arrival. For the
Lord your God is the very God in heaven above and on
earth below.* (Josh 2:9-11)

Twice Rahab mentions in the quote above that in fear her
people melted (*"languished"* Josh 2:9,11). The first use is מוּג,
as Moses and Miriam sung prophetically after they crossed the
Red Sea that *"all the inhabitants of Canaan"* melted away
(Ex 15:15). The second instance is מָסַס, which describes how
the hearts of the Israelites *"melted"* when the spies sent into
Canaan the first time came back with fearful reports of giant
warriors and cities fortified up to heaven (Dt 1:28).[112]

While fear destroys many, Rahab received it as grace, the
fear of the Lord being the beginning of wisdom. She
recognised that the Hebrew God Who dried up a sea, Who
defeated mighty kings in battle, *"is the very God in heaven
above and on earth below"*. She understood Jericho had no
chance to resist Him or His People.

While Rahab perceived God is Almighty, at the same time
she perceived God is Mercy. Because she acted with mercy
toward the two spies, they were duty bound in the Name of
God to act mercifully to her household:

---

[112] Interestingly, it also describes how the manna in the desert *"melted"* once the
sun got hot (Ex 16:21). The proper time to collect the manna was early, so Wisdom
informs us: *"For that which could not be destroyed by fire, was immediately melted
when warmed by a few rays of the sun, so that it might be clear to all that it is right
to come before the sun [rises] to bless you, and to adore you at the dawning of the
light. For the hope of the ungrateful will melt away like the winter's ice and will
disperse like overflowing water"* (Wis 16:27-29). Their hearts melt who do not rise
early to thank God, who are not fortified by the bread of angels (Wis 16:20).

Swear to me by the Lord that in the same way that I have acted with mercy toward you, so also shall you act toward the house of my father. And may you give me a true sign that you will save my father and mother, my brothers and sisters, and all that is theirs, and that you may rescue our souls from death. (Josh 2:12-13)

This is faith! This is the rare greatness which earns Rahab a place in St Paul's list with Abraham and Moses.

In all this Rahab anticipates Our Lady, for the *"two spies"* who came to visit her represent the two natures of Jesus Christ — Divine and human — Whom Our Lady received. As Mediatrix, Mary confidently asks Him to save all her household from (eternal) death: first her *"father and mother"* (being the righteous of Adam and those of the synagogue of Moses before Jesus came), and then her *"brothers and sisters"* (believers baptised in Christ). But how do the two spies represent the Incarnation? The episode begins:

And so Joshua, the son of Nun, sent two men... to explore in secret. And he said to them, 'Go and consider the land and the city of Jericho.' And while traveling, they entered into the house of a harlot woman named Rahab, and they rested with her. (Josh 2:1)

At this time Joshua was the greatest man on the planet — let him represent God. He sends the *"two men"* as the Son of God was sent on His mission in two Natures to redeem the world. The men are to *"explore in secret"*. Here *"explore"* means to be spies, to weigh up *"the land and the city"* for

147

conquest. So Jesus came to conquer the world: our hearts and our minds. חֶרֶשׁ means secretly, silently, even magically, which is how God became present in the womb of the Virgin Mary. They *"entered the house... and rested"* there or *"lodged"* there. She hid them there (Josh 2:6). So the Son of God, hidden, dwelt bodily within Mary.[113]

Sacred Scripture records that Rahab was a *"harlot"*. How can this fit in a prefiguration of the Immaculate Virgin Mary? The word שָׁכַב, *"rested"* at root means "to lie down" or "sleep". Many times in the Torah it indicates corrupted sexual activity.[114] But the first time and the last time and the middle occurrence of this word in Genesis are all holy usages.[115] So in the midst of all those corrupt uses, notably sexual sin, there is holiness found. The two spies *"rested"* or *"lodged"* with Rahab but there was no sin. In Mary the two natures of Christ did dwell, did lodge, but not due to any sexual embrace, rather

---

[113] At the end of the *Salve Regina* we praise God for preparing "the body and soul of Mary, glorious Virgin and Mother, to become a worthy dwelling for Thy Son".

[114] Gen 19:32-35; 26:10; 30:16; 24:2,7; 35:22; 39:7-14. It gets worse in Ex 22:19.

[115] The first use of שָׁכַב is when the two messengers *"lay down"* to rest in Sodom (Gen 19:4). Though the city outside was raging with depravity, they were the two holy angels sent to save those few who could be saved (as our two spies in Jericho did). The middle usage occurs when, in a vision granted to Jacob, *"the Lord, leaning upon the ladder"* promises him that his offspring will inherit the land upon which he is *"sleeping"* (Gen 28:13). The Lord leaning on the ladder signifies the Divinity of Christ at the Crucifixion, while Jacob sleeping on the rock signifies the Humanity of Christ dying at the Crucifixion. Through this action the promised land is inherited. So our two spies resting with Rahab are associated with fulfilling this promise, the beginning of the winning of the Promised Land. And the last usage in Genesis is Jacob's insistent command that he be carried out of Egypt and buried (*"lie"*) with his fathers (Gen 47:30). This may represent the holy souls departing this world to inherit heaven with the saints, entering into God's *"rest"*. This is the full meaning of conquering Jericho, of entering Canaan as the Holy Land: Heaven.

by the message of an angel. In the midst of a fallen world, in the City of Man, God's messengers come, and He Himself comes, to redeem us from it. What begins well will end well.

The two spies were on a mission from God. Of course, they aroused attention for, in those days with the threat of war, all strangers in a city were closely watched. To guard one's identity, the least suspicious place to visit and the most likely place one would be accepted, would be the house of a harlot. Even so, straight away

the king of Jericho sent to Rahab, saying: 'Bring out the men who came to you, and who entered into your house. For certainly they are spies, and they have arrived to consider the entire land.' (Josh 2:3)

The king wanted the two spies found and killed like King Herod hearing of Jesus wanted Him found and killed. Is Jesus a spy? No, but He too kept His identity hidden at the beginning phase of His mission, and He too *"arrived to consider the entire land"*, that is, Jesus came to take for Himself the entire world. The poor king was correct to fear, for the last verse of the chapter tells us:

And crossing the Jordan, they went to Joshua, the son of Nun, and they reported to him all that had happened to them. And they said, 'The Lord has delivered this entire land into our hands, and all its inhabitants have been struck down by fear.' (Josh 2:23-24)

"Crossing the Jordan" means going to the other side of death, so Jesus after His Passion ascends to the Father, confirming

that the mission will be entirely successful. The spies eagerly reported likewise after encountering Rahab: *"The Lord has delivered this entire land into our hands"*. In allegory, God confidently chose to depend upon Mary. He trusted her.

The significance of Rahab being a prostitute is threefold. First, God came to redeem sinners, and He does so successfully. Second, Rahab represents the Church, whom St Ambrose once called a *casta meretrix*, a "chaste whore" — chaste because she is entirely holy, coming from God; a whore because she joins to herself many peoples, with all the world, with whomever comes to her.[116] And third, because again and again Israel has behaved as a זֹנָה and, what is worse, so has the Church. Both have been so unfaithful to God, both have gone after false gods, both devoured their children, both preferred the works of their own hands to that of God. And, amazingly, God has not disdained to come to Israel and come to the Church. How though can we say the Church is all holy? She is holy in her essence, in her divine constitution, in her mysteries, in her sacraments, in her teaching, in her saints. And all the defilement is from man. Immaculate purity dwelt among filth, and the filth did not overcome it.

Under threat, Rahab is shrewd and extremely quick-thinking, arranging the immediate safety of the two men and diverting the danger: *"she caused the men to ascend to the*

---

[116] See Giacomo Cardinal Biffi, *Casta Meretrix: The Chaste Whore* (2001), citing St Ambrose, Commentary on Lk 8:40. Rahab "as a type was a prostitute but as a mystery is the Church, united now to the Gentiles by the sharing of the sacraments." *"Typo meretrix mysterio ecclesia, sacramentorum consortio populis copulata gentilibus."*

roof of her house" (Josh 2:6).[117] In Mary this signifies the dual-nature of Christ being received in the upper parts of her soul where the God-Man is contemplated. The Son descended so we could ascend. With Jesus in her home, Mary's contemplation would have been higher than ever before.

This all achieved, Rahab then instructed the two men:

Climb up to the mountains; otherwise, they may meet you as they are returning. And lie hidden there for three days, until they return. And then you will go on your way. (Josh 2:16)

Did not Jesus go up the mountain (Calvary), and was He not hidden for three days, and did He not return to His Commander across the Jordan (God the Father) without His enemies encountering Him?

When the spies next returned, it would be with the Army of God, like Jesus at His Second Coming, descending with *"trumpets sounding"*, signifying the Last Day (Josh 6:8,13; Mt 24:31; 1 Thes 4:15; Apoc 8:6). Seven times they circled the city, reminding us of the seven angels of the Apocalypse and, by God's blast, the walls of the City of Man fell forthwith. Joshua ordered a destruction of all souls except:

---

[117] The verse continues: *"and she covered them with the stalks of flax that were there"* (Josh 2:6). The *"flax"* is that used in priestly garments and turbans, but not as reported in the Torah for the desert tabernacle, rather those seen by the Prophet Ezekiel in his vision of the heavenly Temple (Ezek 44:17,18). *"Flax"* was also used to measure this mystical Temple (Ezek 44:3). If the two men represent Jesus hidden in Mary, to be *"covered... with flax"* is to put on the measure and garments of heavenly priesthood. In Mary's womb this means Jesus putting on His Flesh, needful for his Priesthood.

May only Rahab the harlot live, with all who are with
her in the house. For she hid the messengers whom we
sent... Then they set fire to the city and all the things
that were within it, except the gold and silver, and the
vessels of brass or of iron, which they consecrated into
the treasury of the Lord. (Josh 6:17,24)

This signifies that all souls adorned by acts of living charity
will endure with an eternal splendour, their treasure gathered
in Heaven (cf. 1 Cor 3:12*ff*).

How had Rahab and her whole household escaped the
doom? The two spies gave her a *"scarlet cord... as a sign"*
(Josh 2:18) to hang from her window. According to the
Church Fathers, it signifies the Most Precious Blood of Our
Lord.[118] To be marked with this scarlet, with grace in baptism,
means being spared when the confrontation comes. Provided,
that is, one has remained within the Church:

And so, gather your father, and mother, and brothers,
and all your family into your house. Whoever will
have exited from the door of your house, his blood
will be on his own head, and we will be uninvolved. But
the blood of all who will be with you in the house shall
fall back upon our own head, if anyone touches them.
(Josh 2:18-19)

Now this *"scarlet [thread]"* (שָׁנִי), which with Rahab is a
sign of salvation, we encounter adorning the tabernacle and

---

[118] St Clement of Rome, *First Letter to the Corinthians*, 12. Also St Augustine,
Enarration on Psalm 86, 5.

the ephod of the high priest (Ex 26:1,36; 28:6), and for purification rites (Lev 14; Heb 9:19), and tied to the horns of the scapegoat before it was led out of Jerusalem to be sacrificed (Lev 16). All these threads mark Jesus' work of Redemption.[119] Gathering, as it were, all these threads together, we read: *"And stripping Him, they put a scarlet cloak about Him"* (Mt 27:28).

For emphasis, summarising the essentials of what we have read so far, we are told later in the Book of Joshua:

> *Yet truly, Joshua caused Rahab the harlot, and her father's household, and all she had, to survive. And they lived in the midst of Israel, even to the present day. For she hid the messengers, whom he had sent to explore Jericho.* (Josh 6:25)

Translated this means God (*"Joshua"*) has redeemed Mary (*"Rahab"*) and the just Jews born before her (*"her father's household"*) and all souls who, before the Last Day, cling to her (*"and all she had"*), that they may live in the Promised Land (*"Israel"*) for eternity (*"even to the present day"*), that is, Heaven; because she received the message of the angel (*"whom [God] had sent"*) and unseen in her womb hid the two natures of Christ, sent to prepare for Judgement upon the City of Man (*"to explore Jericho"*).

---

[119] The first time שָׁנִי appears in the Bible is the red thread tied around the wrist of Tamar's son Zerah (Gen 38:27). He was set to be senior but hesitated to be born, and was overtaken by Perez, who signifies Christ and the New Covenant. Hence the scarlet thread connects Tamar and Rahab. In fact, it is Jesus and Mary who join them. They are companions in St Matthew's genealogy because they have much in common in their conceiving and achieving, just as Mary does for Jesus.

Or why else were those words even written and preserved by the Jews and the Church? They were written because in their literal sense they are true and good. They were preserved because in their spiritual sense they express a far higher, salvific truth and goodness: if Mary had not received Jesus, True God and True Man (as Rahab received the two spies), then nobody in the world could be saved.

In the next section we see how Mary takes care not only of the big picture, of the whole household, but also of the details, of individual souls.

Ruth: That Not One Be Lost

Regarding Ruth, her first husband, Mahlon, died after ten years of marriage, leaving her childless (Rth 1:5). They lived in Moab, but he was originally from Bethlehem, of the tribe of Ephraim. Some feared Ruth would never find another husband if she came to Israel, for the Moabites were despised. But there Ruth wedded Mahlon's kinsman, *"a powerful man, and very wealthy, named Boaz"* (Rth 2:1). He too was of Bethlehem, of the elect tribe of Judah, and through this union Ruth became great-grandmother to King David. That Judah has a more favoured status than Ephraim we hear from the Psalmist singing of God:

> *And he rejected the tabernacle of Joseph, and he did not choose the tribe of Ephraim. But he chose the tribe of Judah: Mount Zion, which he loved.* (Ps 77:67-68)

Evidently, Ruth conceived by a man greater than her first husband Mahlon (whose name means "sickness").

Receiving great favour from Boaz, Ruth wonders with words still more suitable for Mary:

> *I have found grace in thy eyes, my lord, who hast comforted me, and hast spoken to the heart of thy handmaid, who am not like to one of thy maids.* (Rth 2:13 DRB)

Like Mary at the Annunciation, Ruth refers to her *"lord"* (אֲדֹנִי , κύριε, *domine*), calls herself *"thy handmaid"* (*ancillæ tuæ* cf. Lk 1:38), and certainly she is not like other maids of the Lord, that is other souls, for Mary is Immaculately

Conceived. Therefore *"the Lord gave her to conceive, and to bear a son"* (Rth 4:13; cf. Lk 1:31).

That Ruth foreshadows Our Lady's victory over satan is not in explicitly crushing anyone's head, but something more subtle. Central to the story of Ruth is the threshing floor where she joined Boaz sleeping. Here the pair prefigure the Crucifixion, where the wheat is separated from the chaff, the souls of the blessed are discerned from the damned. The main action of the Book of Ruth takes place at harvest time. This is a figure of the end times, for Jesus spoke of it in parables, saying *"gather the wheat into my barn"*, stating *"truly, the harvest is the consummation of the age; while the reapers are the Angels"* (Mt 13:30, 39; cf. Mt 9:37-38; Jn 4:35). This key shines a new light on the Book of Ruth. The grain represents souls; the reapers the angels. Boaz is Christ and his field is the Church. Ruth represents Our Lady with her care for souls and of whom the angels speak:

> *And behold, he came out of Bethlehem and said to the reapers, 'The Lord be with you' ...And Boaz said to the young man who was in charge of the reapers, 'Whose young woman is this?' He answered him, 'This is the Moabite woman... and she asked to gather the remnants of the ears of grain, following the steps of the reapers, and from morning until now she has remained in the field, and, indeed, not for one moment has she returned home.' And Boaz said to Ruth, 'Listen to me, daughter. Do not go to gather in any other field... I have given orders to my young men, so that no one is to harass you.*

*And so, whenever you are thirsty, go to the vessels, and
drink from the waters that the young men also drink.'
She, falling on her face and paying homage on the
ground...* (Rth 2:4-10)

With the reapers representing the angels, then the *"young
man who was in charge of the reapers"* represents the angels'
commander-in-chief, St Michael. The Church sings on his
feast: "Michael mine Archangel, I have appointed thee for a
prince over the ingathering of souls."[120] Boaz gives the angels
orders to protect Ruth as the Lord ensures protection for Mary.
Boaz tells Ruth: *"whenever you are thirsty... drink from the
waters that the young men also drink"*, for Our Lady is Queen
of Angels, and her soul drinks pure truth like they do. In
humility she falls down and worships.

Moreover, Ruth came to Bethlehem at the beginning of the
reaping ("εἰς Βαιθλεεμ ἐν ἀρχῇ θερισμοῦ" Rth 1:22). Mary's
arrival in Bethlehem points to the beginning of the harvest of
souls, the shepherds and wise men being the first gleanings,
and the Holy Innocents the first sheaves of angelic reaping.

While the reapers take in great armloads of sheaves, Ruth
painstakingly gleans. She searches for individual grains which
other harvesters have left behind. Working without pause
"from morning until now", Ruth *"continued to glean with
them, till all the barley and the wheat were laid up in the
barns"* (Rth 2:23 DRB). So does our Blessed Mother
assiduously seek and gather souls for Heaven, bringing the

---

[120] Michaelmas, Vespers I, Antiphon III: *"Archangele Míchaël, constitui te principem
super omnes animas suscipiendas."*

157

least of us to the Lord of the Harvest, God.[121] If in self-doubt we suppose we are too insignificant for Mary's close attention, Ruth can convince us otherwise. Ruth and Mary work like Jesus: *"that not one be lost"* (Jn 6:12; 6:39; 17:12; 18:9). God's victory is total.

The devil knows he cannot defeat God. He has long discovered he cannot keep humans out of Heaven. But if he could get one, just one of the elect, then in all his misery he would have some satisfaction. Yes, he is filling hell fast with countless souls but none mean anything to him as booty, for they are the godless who could not bear to be in Heaven anyway. None of them honour the Mother of God. What would suit satan is to capture a soul for whom God made a place in Heaven. If he could get someone who loved Our Lady as their own mother, then he would sting her too. But he cannot. Mary is too careful, too attentive to detail, too willing to labour, too determined, and all this to the end of time:

> *And so she gathered in the field until evening. And striking and threshing with a staff what she had gathered, she found about the measure of an ephah of barley, that is, three measures.* (Rth 2:17)

Does this verse say one measure or three? A measure for God is equal to a measure for the Father, and for the Son and for the Holy Spirit, One and Three.

---

[121] Jesus compares gathering souls to a harvest (Mt 9:38; Lk 10:2). St Clement of Rome writes of God's chastening mercy: "You will go down into the grave like ripened corn to be harvested at the right time, or like a heap on the threshing-floor that is garnered at the appointed time" (*First Letter to the Corinthians*, 56).

Honouring God, Ruth also rescued her own people. Moab had been conceived in great shame (Gen 19:31-27). But Ruth, being a Moabitess with a book of the Bible named after her, as the great-grandmother of King David and remote mother of Jesus Christ the Saviour of the World, single-handedly rehabilitates the reputation of the Moabites, as excellent Achior did for their Ammonite cousins (whereof we read in Judith). The sins of Lot's daughters were no longer the main story. Another sting for satan.

Finally, Ruth had great faith in the Living God. Consider this exchange between her despondent mother-in-law, Naomi, representing the synagogue of Moses reaching an age of sterility, and in contrast Ruth, young and hopeful, who counted fidelity higher than progeny and, thereby, won all. It is one of several passages in the short book which illustrate Ruth's nature was close to perfect. How selfless was Ruth's response when Naomi said:

> *'Return, my daughters. Why come with me? Do I have any more sons in my womb, so that you could hope for husbands from me? Return, my daughters, go forth. For I am now exhausted by old age, and not fit for the bond of marriage... your difficulties weigh upon me greatly, and the hand of the Lord has been set against me.' In response... Ruth clung to her mother-in-law. Naomi said to her, 'See, your kinswoman [Orpah] returns to her people, and to her gods. Hurry after her.' She answered, 'Do not be against me, as if I would abandon you and go away; for wherever you will go, I will go, and where*

you will stay, I also will stay with you. Your people are my people, and your God is my God. Whichever land will receive you dying, in the same I will die, and there I will have the place of my burial'... And so they set out together, and they came to Bethlehem... [Naomi said to the women there] 'Do not call me Naomi (that is, beautiful), but call me Mara (that is, bitter). For the Almighty has greatly filled me with bitterness. I went out full and the Lord led me back empty. So then, why call me Naomi, whom the Lord has humbled and the Almighty has afflicted?' Therefore, Naomi went with Ruth, the Moabite, her daughter-in-law, from the land of her sojourn, and returned to Bethlehem, at the time of the first reaping of the barley. (Rth 1:11-22)

By having hope Ruth rescued the world, keeping alive the messianic line running from Abraham to David. And she gave joy to her mother-in-law, Naomi, as one day the Church will do for the Jews, the young one saying to the elder: *"your God is my God"*. In the very end the two, Jews and Gentiles, will go together to Bethlehem, or rather to the place of the Advent of the Lord, His Second Advent that is, His Second Coming at the time of the *"reaping of the barley"*. Not one of the elect will be lost. In God's Plan every soul matters.

The depiction of Ruth as one who carefully gleans grains is as important for the final victory as that of her OT sisters who sit with an emperor, hurl millstones from towers, arrange summary beheadings or themselves wield the sword. How enormous is the fruit of diligent work. It is this that attracted

Boaz to Ruth. And how vital it turned out to be for us all that Ruth and he had a child. St Augustine wonders whether or not Ruth remarried because she knew in faith that it would serve Christ coming into the world.[122]

In fact this is a task of all mothers, an opportunity to share in the work of Our Lady. Much of Mary's victory will come through those devoted to her in the slow and humble work of raising children to God. The virtues practised here are many. They include purity and fidelity which strengthen marriage, generosity in openness to life, constancy and self-sacrifice in caring unselfishly daily for decades for children — helpless little ones, sensitive young ones, vulnerable teenagers. Above all, their imparting the virtue of religion in bringing these up to pray, to know the Bible, to live sacramentally. In this way Christ is brought into the world, in the souls of the baptised who live in grace.

Thanks to the many mothers who do all this, there are armies of Catholics coming through, notably from large tradition-loving families. Women who cannot bear children can always be fruitful in the better part, spiritually ripening many souls for the Lord's harvest, even carefully gleaning those who would otherwise be overlooked. Meanwhile, the Antichrist's team is sterile, dying out in the culture of death. This is why they are so thirsty to corrupt children.

Now there is a danger when gleaning the Word of God for details that being too assiduous one gathers chaff instead of truth. But there are delicate threads running through Ruth's

---

[122] St Augustine, *On the Good of Widowhood*, X.

story which connect with Tamar and Rahab. I think they are wheat, fit for our spiritual nourishment.

Naomi had said:

> *Turn back, my daughters, go your way, for I am too old to have a husband. If I should say I have hope, even if I should have a husband this night and should bear sons...* (Rth 1:12 RSVCE).

This word for *"hope"* — תִּקְוָה — is the same as that used for the scarlet *"cord"* hung from Rahab's window (Josh 2:18,21). It is used dozens of times to mean hope, longing, expectation, but only once does it mean *"cord"*, there in Joshua as a sign of Jesus' Passion.[123] Is not His Passion the hope and expectation of the world, the thread running through time from Creation to Apocalypse, hung from the window which is the portal between the natural world and the supernatural? We are to see through this from the world of frantic externals to the inner place of peace, to go from the accidents to the substance, the sensible to the ineffable. The scarlet of the Passion marks this way from the dangerous city into the peaceful household of Our Lady, into God's House. Naomi does not know she has hope through her "daughter" Ruth. So those who still think with the Old Covenant do not yet realise their hope lies in Mary, in the Son she bears.

---

[123] It is a mysterious phrase. In the Septuagint the word used is ὑπόστασις, which means substance or person. It is the fundamental reality, "standing-under" (ὑπό-στασις, *sub-stans*) everything we perceive. Theologically speaking, there are three ὑποστάσεις, three Persons, in the Holy Trinity. The Latin has something different again: *"nec apta vinculo conjugali"*, *"not fit for the bond of marriage"* (Rth 1:12).

We recall too that Tamar's son Zerah, brother of Perez, had a שָׁנִי, a *"scarlet"* thread tied around his wrist before birth (Gen 38:28,30). When the people and elders of Bethlehem saw Ruth's goodness, they cried out to Boaz:

And may your house be like the house of Perez, whom Tamar bore to Judah, of the offspring which the Lord will give to you from this young woman. (Rth 4:12)

They desire Ruth to bear to Boaz a son not like Zerah, but like Perez, that is one who will surprise everyone by taking the birthright which seemed to be owed to another.[124] This was fulfilled in Ruth's eventual Son Jesus, the desired *"offspring"*, Who establishing the New Covenant gained for His House the eternal inheritance of the Father.

Alluding to the same salvific purpose, previously Boaz had called all present to witness that he married Ruth

to raise up the name of the deceased [Mahlon] in his posterity, so his name will not be cut off from among his family and his brethren and his people. (Rth 4:10)

This union of Boaz and Ruth was to heal the sick (recalling Mahlon's name means "sickness"), even to raise the dead, as it were. That is, to ensure that Mahlon would be remembered in the land of the living — a way of expressing heaven. Again it is Jesus Who achieves all this in full. He is there for every

---

[124] The context for the crowd's jubilation was that although there was a kinsman higher in rank to marry Ruth, he forewent this privilege (duty), so Boaz came through and married her (see Rth 4:1-10). Correspondingly, the elder brother Zerah, positioned first in the womb, withdrew his hand and himself and thereby lost the birthright.

soul. The diametrical opposite of having Heaven's foot crush one's skull is having one's head lovingly supported by the hand of the Beloved Lord: *"For I languish through love. His left hand is under my head, and his right hand shall embrace me"* (Cant 2:5-6).

Or why does the OT use *"cords"* and *"thread"* and *"hope"* to link Rahab, Tamar and Ruth, except that the hanging cord, the scarlet thread, the expectant hope, are all for Jesus Christ? This is even more obvious at the end of the Book of Ruth. The three women — Tamar, Rahab and Ruth — are implicitly linked in a genealogy. This was an important record for the Book's author, possibly the Prophet Samuel, to show the continuum from the era of judges to that of kings. So the Book opens: *"In the days of one of the judges, when the judges ruled"* (Rth 1:1). And the Book closes with the name of Israel's greatest king until Jesus:

> *These are the generations of Perez: Perez begot Hezron, Hezron begot Aram, Aram begot Amminadab, Amminadab begot Nahshon, Nahshon begot Salmon, Salmon begot Boaz, Boaz begot Obed, Obed begot Jesse, Jesse begot David.* (Rth 4:18-22)[125]

We can compare it to St Matthew's genealogy:

> *And Judah begot Perez and Zerah by Tamar. And Perez begot Hezron. And Hezron begot Ram. And Ram begot Amminadab. And Amminadab begot Nahshon. And*

---

[125] In this quote and the next *"begot"* (DRB) is repeatedly used to replace *"conceived"*.

Nahshon begot Salmon. And Salmon begot Boaz by Rahab. And Boaz begot Obed by Ruth. And Obed begot Jesse. And Jesse begot king David. And king David begot Solomon, by her who had been the wife of Uriah.
(Mt 1:3-6)

St Matthew, inspired by the Holy Spirit, kept a faithful record. Without giving more information here than the OT already contains, he draws our attention to Tamar, Rahab, Ruth and to *"her who had been the wife of Uriah"*. The Evangelist has definite reasons for doing this. He wants to convince us of something vital. The Spirit wants to convince us.

If three examples so far of admirable conceiving and crucial achieving have not been enough, maybe a fourth example, Bathsheba, will persuade of the Marian link.

BATHSHEBA: יחי אדני המלך דוד לעלם

The chief quality of Bathsheba is blindingly obvious, at least to men: she was gorgeous; stunning to behold; jaw-dropping. As numberless works of art try to attest, seeing her a man's mind would go blank. Gazing voyeuristically from a rooftop on bathing Bathsheba, King David forgot himself, forgot his heroic companions, and finally forgot God (2 Sam 11:2-4).

What has this to do with the Virgin Mary? Mary — the Mystical Rose, House of Gold, Morning Star — was beautiful, but not in a way Hollywood could recognise. Mary, the most beautiful of creatures, did nothing to evoke sexual interest in any man. Still, Bathsheba points to Mary because if we remove from the scenario everything carnal, if we retain only the ideas of attraction and desire for self-gift, then we have an inkling of how much God loves holiness when He sees it, how attracted God is to Mary's pure soul. Given the soul of Our Lady is immaculate, without any stain of sin, full of grace, then we have data to meditate upon in considering how much stronger God's love for Mary is than David's passion for Bathsheba.

May we not think of God, when all this happened, as we read David was walking *"on the roof of the house of the king"* (*"in solario domus regiae"* 2 Sam 11:2)? It sounds heavenly: the poetic cadence; the elevated and exclusive location; the leisurely pace; and the *"solario"* — terrace of the sun. It is a vantage point fit for God.

Some propose that Bathsheba was not simply bathing, but performing the ritual washing enjoined by Moses. Thus she was pure through keeping the Law. Might this not speak of Mary also? What else would inflame God's dilection for His creature except that she be fulfilling His Law, His Will?

How strongly God is attracted to our souls if they are purified of sin by baptism and by confession. If we offer sacrifices to God with devotion, this interests Him more than any woman ever interested any man. If we mortify ourselves, His heart melts. If we humble ourselves before Him then we become, as it were, irresistible to Him. Of course He loves us even when we are sinners — or else we would not exist. But that is the love of our Creator. Beyond this, He wants to live inside us as Lover. And most of us are so troubled by self-doubt and insecurity or even such disgust at our own sins that we cannot hold onto this truth for long, that God loves us more than we can imagine. Maybe Bathsheba's effect on David can help convince us?

Bathsheba was married to Uriah, an exceedingly virtuous and heroic Hittite, so brave in battle he attained to being counted as *"one of the thirty"* (1 Chron 11:25,41). But like the other three women in this section, Bathsheba points to Mary in that she conceived by one greater than her husband. Impressive as Uriah was, Bathsheba became pregnant by David, a war hero since his youth, not merely *"one of the thirty"* but the very one who chose them, the King of all Israel, pre-eminent figure in the OT of God's Anointed, Christ the prophetic King. Prescinding from David's major moral lapse, undoubtedly Bathsheba conceived by one greater than her husband.

This is not to say the moral aspect is overlooked. The Prophet Nathan provoked a profound repentance from King David for attempting to hide adultery through homicide:

> *why have you despised the word of the Lord, so that you did evil in my sight? You have struck down Uriah the Hittite with the sword. And you have taken his wife as a wife for yourself. And you have put him to death with the sword of the sons of Ammon.* (2 Sam 12:9)

The chroniclers of Israel's history were wonderfully honest:

> *For David had done what was right in the eyes of the Lord, and he had not declined from all of the things that he had instructed to him, during all the days of his life, except the matter of Uriah, the Hittite.* (1 Kngs 15:5)

David admitted his fault and he prayerfully accepted a grievous penance from God's Hand: his firstborn by Bathsheba died (2 Sam 12:15-24). Hence Bathsheba, too, indirectly representing Mary, knew the death of her firstborn son. Following this, David, in the most profound contrition, gave us Psalm 50, the *Miserere*, which has helped to rescue millions of sinners from despair ever since.

It may seem that, out of sensitivity to this scandalous sin, while Tamar, Rahab and Ruth are all named in St Matthew's genealogy, Bathsheba is referred to only indirectly: *"And king David conceived Solomon, by her who had been the wife of Uriah"* (Mt 1:6).

But we need not think St Matthew was squeamish about mentioning her who had been party to this crime. Bathsheba mourned her husband sincerely (2 Sam 11:26). And who knows if Bathsheba does not suffer with the Virgin Mary by being suspected of sin where she is innocent? For centuries Mary has been calumniated by men who do not believe in the Virgin birth. Perhaps Bathsheba is calumniated, too, by people making assumptions about her actions?

In any case, St Matthew honours Uriah by mentioning him in this list while Our Lady's humility is hinted at by Bathsheba's anonymity. Most importantly, St Matthew draws our attention to the triangular relation between David, Bathsheba and Uriah, so we might recall that this is the fourth woman in the list who conceived by a man greater than her supposed husband. The explicit connection would fail if he did not mention Uriah, for had St Matthew only written: "And king David conceived Solomon, and Solomon conceived Rehoboam" (cf. Mt 1:6-7), then there is nothing of the prefiguration here, because by that time David and Bathsheba were lawfully married.

In all this St Augustine uncovers a mystery. He sees Bathsheba as a type of the Church, with King David in the place of Christ and Uriah as a figure for the devil.[126] Christ wins all His chosen souls from the devil, as David takes Bathsheba from Uriah. It may surprise us that in the story involving his most heinous act, King David is seen to prefigure Christ. Likewise that a man so outstanding in

---

[126] St Augustine, *Contra Faustum*, XXII, 87.

goodness as Uriah is taken as a figure for the devil. But such a photographic negative — showing light as darkness and darkness as light — is another way for God to portray an important image (as with the Shroud of Turin).

Having prefigured the Annunciation and the espousal of the Church to Christ, do we find with Bathsheba some prefiguration also of Mary's triumph? Yes. Some twenty years later Queen Bathsheba, taking counsel from the prophet Nathan, secured the whole kingdom for her son Solomon as David had promised it should be (1 Kngs 1:17,30). Thereby Bathsheba speaks also to the end times.

In happened like this. Toward the end of David's life one of his elder sons (by another wife), Adonijah, sought to seize the kingdom for himself. Here he represents the Antichrist — an attractive but rebel royal who sets up a parallel administration and offers bloody sacrifices at the satanically sounding *"Stone of the Serpent"* (1 Kngs 1:9). He does this while seeking to usurp the messianic throne from his younger brother, Solomon. His attempt failed. While Adonijah's hubris caused his own downfall, Bathsheba was instrumental both in ensuring the throne for Solomon and in the execution of his rival (1 Kngs 2:13*ff*).

Mirroring Mary's uniquely close relation to the Blessed Trinity, Bathsheba achieved this double-sided victory through her closeness to a father, spirit and son. The first part, securing her son's throne, was won by her intercession with the father (King David: 1 Kngs 1:15-31), through an inspiration from the spirit of his royal court (given through Nathan the Prophet:

1 Kngs 1:11-14); the second part, the eradication of evil, was gained by Bathsheba's audience with the son (King Solomon: 1 Kngs 2:13-25), that is, the son of David, son of the father.

In the account, King David was very old and did not know how to deal with the insurrection without Bathsheba's firm focus. The Prophet Nathan had said to her: *"come, accept my counsel, and save your life and the life of your son Solomon"* (1 Kngs 1:12). This Bathsheba obediently did, and thereby kept salvation history on course. As a young man, Solomon prayed for wisdom, and through this humility and gift, he was able to have a House built for the Lord exactly as David had commissioned him. It was humanly impossible for his elder brother Adonijah to do this, whose thoughts were much more for his own glory and pleasure.

Though David loved Bathsheba with a passion in the early years, it still required courage from her to approach him on these matters at the end of his life. It could be dangerous to make a request of the king uninvited. And David loved his other sons despite their gross crimes — including Ammon's incestuous rape of David's daughter and Absalom's usurpation of David's throne (2 Sam 13-15). Perhaps David might have favoured Adonijah? But Bathsheba reminded him of his promise for their son Solomon, and David honourably kept it for the sake of his promise — even as God maintains mercy on Israel for the sake of His own Name and the promises He made to Abraham, Issac and Jacob.

This all achieved:

Bathsheba, having lowered her face to the ground, reverenced the king, saying — יְחִי אֲדֹנִי הַמֶּלֶךְ דָּוִד לְעֹלָם — *'May my lord David live forever'.* (1 Kngs 1:31)

Her petition is fulfilled in Jesus Christ.

As for seeing to Adonijah's execution, there is little reason to suppose that Bathsheba did not know in advance precisely what the result would be of her passing on his request to King Solomon, that he be given his father David's virgin helpmate, Abishag (1 Kngs 1:1-4), as a wife. In this, Adonijah is like the Antichrist who strains to take Christ's Virgin Bride, the Church, for his own. The usurper's ambition was resurgent; he was still trying to seize the kingdom; Solomon had him put to death the same day (1 Kngs 2:17-25).

After this, the ancient nation of Israel began what would be counted as the best few years of its life, building a House for God wherein He would dwell among them. They would be the best years until, in ancient Israel's twilight, God came not only in a glorious cloud, but actually arrived in the Flesh.

IV: A HIDDEN ARROW POINTING TO ST JOSEPH

I f we are fully satisfied that the four great, great-grandmothers of Jesus of the previous section point in their various ways to the Mother of God — partly because all four were crucial to God's providential plan for the salvation of the world, but more specifically in that each conceived by persons higher than their supposed husbands — then, on this basis, we can find St Joseph indicated too. If we identify the reasons why the women named in the genealogy did not conceive by the person one might have expected, we discover an exponentially positive development in the character of these supposed husbands.

Tamar did not conceive by Er, nor by Onan, nor by Shelah. The series culminated in a certain distance between the spouses. Er doubtless wished to impregnate Tamar, but was not worthy (*"Er, the first born of Judah, was wicked in the sight of the Lord and was killed by him"* Gen 38:7). Onan had a certain ardour for Tamar but was unwilling to raise children for his dead brother, so *"he spilled his seed on the ground... [and] the Lord struck him down, because he did a detestable thing"* (Gen 38:9-10). Shelah, by a decision of the father (Judah), had no spousal relations at all.

In Rahab's case, no mention of children is ever made until she marries Salmon. Whatever relations went before this, apparently they were providentially childless. Yet those men who went before Salmon had given Rahab, by their payments, her means of livelihood which fulfils at least some contract (overlooking the overall immorality of prostitution). Until now the analogy with St Joseph has barely gotten off the ground.

In Ruth's story, if we take Boaz to figure God and Ruth to figure Mary, we find words which point to St Joseph. Boaz said to Ruth:

Neither do I deny myself to be a near relative, but there is another nearer than I. Be at peace for this night. And when morning arrives, if he is willing to uphold the law of kinship for you, things will turn out well; but if he is not willing, then, I will take you, without any doubt, as the Lord lives. Sleep until morning. (Rth 3:12-13)

174

This *"nearer kinsman"* did not embrace Ruth maritally. He represents St Joseph, a blood relative of Mary who in a real sense is closer to her than to God. Although God is closer to each one of us than we are to ourselves, it is also a fact that the difference between the Blessed Virgin Mary and St Joseph is emphatically minor in comparison to the infinite gap between the Virgin Mary and God, for before Him we are all next to nothing. In this sense St Joseph is closer to Mary. In perfect freedom this kinsman answered Boaz:

> *I yield my right of kinship, for I am obliged not to cut off the posterity of my own family. You may make use of my privilege, which I freely declare I will forego.* (Rth 4:6)

Thus did this closer kinsman decide not to take Ruth, but to let Boaz, the distant father of Jesus, do so. Likewise, St Joseph surrendered paternal generation with Mary to the distant Father of Jesus, God Himself.[127]

Finally, we consider Uriah the Hittite: a virtuous man; a hero; *"one of the thirty"* (2 Sam 23:39; 1 Chron 11:41). His fortitude in battle was outstanding, as was his obedience, coming and going immediately as ordered. In all this he is like St Joseph. But most strikingly, Uriah is a model of chastity, who with good reason refused to sleep with his own wife, nor even would he lie down with her (2 Sam 11), saying to David:

---

[127] Boaz spoke to this kinsman, *"calling him by his name"* (Rth 4:1). We may think of God addressing St Joseph personally through angels and dreams. Parenthetically, the deal was sealed when *"Boaz said to his kinsman: Put off your shoe. And immediately he took it off from his foot"* (Rth 4:8): one thinks of Moses and Joshua approaching holy ground; perhaps also St Joseph, living so close to the true burning bush and ark of the covenant.

The ark of God, and Israel and Judah, dwell in tents, and my lord Joab, and the servants of my lord, stay upon the face of the earth. And should I then go into my own house, so that I may eat and drink, and sleep with my wife? By your welfare and by the welfare of your soul, I will not do this thing. (2 Sam 11:11)

Bathsheba was a stunningly good-looking woman yet Uriah showed a saintly restraint, motivated by an honourable love for God, for his commander in the field and his fellow warriors.

If we take these four cases separately, then it strains credibility to see St Joseph unambiguously figured in any of them: the tragic husbands of Tamar; the shameless clients of Rahab; the perhaps selfish kinsman of Ruth; and not even, if taken alone, the awesome Uriah. But taken as a series, there is a development to be discovered which certainly points to the highest and holiest of souls.

The respective reasons each had for refusing to father children begins with a baseness *contra naturam* (Onan could have been a progenitor of Christ if he were not such a... an onanist); through to fornication which is gravely sinful but not against nature;[128] ascending to an honourable and legal refusal to marry (knowing a beloved man was waiting and willing); and attaining in Uriah to outstanding virtue, who refused to entertain the slightest temptation, preferring to serve the good of his people. In this five-century ascent from grave sin to a

---

[128] St Thomas, *S.Th.* II-II, Q.154 a.12.

lesser sin to social decency then sanctity, we find an arrow traced pointing upward to holiness; an ascent needing a whole millennium more until it could suitably designate St Joseph, the holiest of men there has been.

At the foot of the arrow the refusal by Tamar's spouses to generate children was for sinful reasons. At the tip of the arrow in the case of Joseph and Mary, their restraint was perfectly willed, the biological sacrificed for the sake of the spiritual. By this holy sacrifice there was a far greater multiplication of life, eternal life, than could have been by any other decision.

If this arrow is rather hidden, that is fitting for St Joseph, the most humble of men. He was the greatest man on the planet, spending more years in Jesus' company than any other male, and yet he does not say a single word in Scripture. He is content to be silent, but if we seek him, we may find him — and in the following section, indisputably so.

ST JOSEPH IN JOSEPH, AND BOTH IN CHRIST

Jesus Christ is present on every page of the Old Testament. Variously He is foreshadowed, prophesied, seen obscurely in a vision or appears in a theophany, for example, as the Angel of the Lord. His Passion is prefigured countless times, as are the Sacraments He instituted. And, as related to Him, His Mother, His saints, His Kingdom and His Cross are alluded to throughout. Unsurprisingly, this list includes Christ's adoptive father, St Joseph. If the hidden arrow outlined above is too faint, here we will examine an unmistakable type of St Joseph, one wonderfully celebrated in the Church's liturgy. Where we find St Joseph we find Jesus, for Jesus is the life of the saints.

The Office of Matins on the Feast of St Joseph Spouse of the Blessed Virgin Mary (19th March), drawing on the insights of the Fathers', celebrates numerous ways in which St Joseph is prefigured in Genesis by Joseph the "great Patriarch who was sold into Egypt".[129] In the second nocturn, St Bernard preaches that the second Joseph not only received the name of the first, "but inherited his purity, and was likened to him in innocence and in grace".[130] Despite relentless attempts by Potiphar's wife to seduce him:

---

[129] Similar insights are given by St Bernadino of Siena, recalled in the Matins of the Solemnity of St Joseph Patron of the Universal Church (pre-1955, kept on the Wednesday before the Third Sunday after Easter).

[130] *Lectiones* IV-VI are taken from St Bernard, Abbot of Clairvaux, *Sermon II on Lk 1:26.* Here Joseph of Egypt is seen to point both directly to Christ and also to St Joseph Spouse of the Blessed Virgin Mary.

that first Joseph kept loyal to his master, and would not carnally know his master's wife; that second Joseph knew that the Lady, the Mother of his Lord, was a virgin, and he himself remained faithfully virgin toward her.

Made receptive by the purity of their souls, both Josephs were informed by God through dreams to serve the salvation of the world. Both went down into Egypt so that God's Firstborn would be called out of there — the first Joseph drawing God's Firstborn nation, Israel, into Egypt; and the second Joseph carrying God's Only Begotten Son Jesus.[131] The Mellifluous Doctor continues: "The first Joseph laid by bread, not for himself, but for all people; the second Joseph received into his keeping that Living Bread Which came down from heaven, not for him only, but for the whole world."[132]

St Bernard notes the two men share a name, יוֹסֵף, which signifies 'Yahweh shall increase'. God had created both precisely to grow in divine life themselves, and to provide for the increase of life of others. This gracious determination is attested by the three scriptural readings (and their responsories) of the first nocturn of Matins, carefully selected from Gen 39:1-5, Gen 41:37-40 and Gen 41:41-44, to illustrate their providential ascents. The first reading tells us:

---

[131] *Responsorium* V: "Arise, and take the young Child and His mother, and flee into Egypt; And be thou there until I bring thee word. That it might be fulfilled which was spoken of the Lord by the Prophet, saying Out of Egypt have I called My Son."

[132] *Responsorium* III: "The Lord hath made me as a father to Pharaoh, and lord of all his house, fear not: For God sent me before you into Egypt, to save your lives."

And the Lord was with him, and he was a man who prospered in everything that he did. And he lived in the house of his lord, who knew very well that the Lord was with him, and that all the things that were done by him were directed by his hand. And Joseph found favour in the sight of his lord, and he ministered to him. And, having been placed in charge of everything by him, he governed the house that was entrusted to him and all the things that had been delivered to him. (Gen 39:2-4)

While the phrase *"the Lord was with him"* is true of the first Joseph, how much more of the second Joseph, who *"lived in the house of his [L]ord"*. How he *"ministered to [H]im"*! How he *"governed the house that was entrusted to him"*. Following this, the first responsory acknowledges that Joseph's 'increase' was given by God and could not be stopped even by imprisonment.[133] Then the second reading shows further increase under Pharaoh, who said to Joseph:

Would we be able to find another such man, who is full of the Spirit of God? ... Because God has revealed to you all that you have said, would I be able to find anyone wiser and as much like you? You will be over my house, and to the authority of your mouth, all the people will show obedience. (Gen 41:38-40)

---

[133] *Responsorium* I: "The Lord was with Joseph, and gave him favour in the sight of the keeper of the prison. And the keeper of the prison committed to Joseph's hand all the prisoners that were in the prison. And whatsoever they did there, he was the doer of it because the Lord was with him, and that which he did, the Lord made it to prosper."

Such progress of favour (advancing from charge over Potiphar's house to Pharaoh's) we see in the life of the second Joseph: first by Holy Matrimony he was appointed to be head of the Blessed Virgin Mary; and then by the birth of Jesus is given custody of the God-Man Himself. Hence the words which the Psalmist sang of the first Joseph are aptly co-opted by the Church for the second St Joseph, positioning them at the end of his litany: *"He made him the lord of his household, And prince over all his possessions"* (cf. Ps 104:21). Truly God set St Joseph as *"prince over all his possessions"* — even His Son was subject to him (Lk 2:51).

Given that Jesus obeyed Joseph, shall not we? Fittingly, the second responsory quotes Pharaoh addressing all of us on God's behalf: *"Go to Joseph. And do whatever he will tell you"* (Gen 41:55). *Ite ad Ioseph!*[134]

The increase did not cease there. In the third reading, again speaking for God, *"Pharaoh said to Joseph, 'Behold, I have appointed you over the entire land of Egypt'..."* (Gen 41:41). Thus as the first Joseph was made head of Pharaoh's household and then the entire land of Egypt, so St Joseph was appointed Head of the Holy Family then honoured in 1870 as Patron of the Universal Church. The gradual unfolding is coherent: St Joseph was set over the sacred household of Nazareth which contained the formal and material principles of the Church, these are respectively the Logos (Son of God)

---

[134] *Responsorium* II: "When all the land of Egypt was famished, the people cried to the king for bread. And the king said unto all the Egyptians: Go unto Joseph [*Ite ad Ioseph*]; and what he saith to you, do."

and the Immaculate Conception (Mother of the Church); therefore he is rightly recognised as chief Patron of the Universal Church.

God and His Church want us to link the two men in our understanding and in our prayers. Both men are named Joseph son of Jacob (Gen 30:24; Mt 1:16). The Litany to the second St Joseph indirectly pays honour to the first in the salutations: *"Joseph castissime, Joseph prudentissime... Speculum patientiæ... Familiarum columen..."* Importantly, the title *"Lumen Patriarcharum"* shows the second is greater than the first, for the second illumines the first.

The OT saints, believing in God's promises, yearned for and strained toward Christ. Humility, chastity, suffering, obedience and even dreams were ways to apprehend Christ. God made St Joseph a repository, a master of these gifts. To attain them is to attain him, and through him to approach closer to Christ. OT Joseph achieved this in anticipation; we are called to the same goal by remembering.

Obviously, to know something of Jesus, Mary and Joseph from the NT, and then to discover these same persons so richly figured in the OT, and their interrelations so finely portrayed, is a phenomenon which pleads for an explanation. It were absurd to suggest all this is a clever artifice of mortals, even the biblical authors. Such a collaboration, stretching over centuries and empires, is beyond the wit or powers of man. However, a perfectly sufficient explanation is supplied if we accept two truths of faith: first, that the Sacred Scriptures are a faithful historical record; and second, that all reality has its single source in God. Together, these two facts explain why there are inexhaustible harmonies to be found within the Scriptures, so many layers comprising coherent unities. Harmony and coherence are found in creation, therefore are found also in the inspired books which describe that creation accurately, with its focus on the most significant aspects.

St Joseph surely knew this, that the ancient Scriptures speak to the present and help those who hear the Word. When St Joseph was confused over Mary's virginal conception of Jesus, when he could find no inn for the birth in Bethlehem, when he was forced to flee with the holy infant to Egypt, when he lost the boy Jesus for three days after the Feast, in all difficulties did he take heart by recalling his namesake Joseph? Was St Joseph consoled by reading of Joseph in Genesis, seeing that God's Plan succeeded in every circumstance? Whether His saints are honoured in their families or hated by them, cast in a pit or promoted by the super-rich, unjustly imprisoned or appointed to the pinnacle of power, both in abundance and in famine, God's Purpose is never deflected. The first Joseph served the second, and the second respected the first. So the bonds in the communion of saints were woven from the earliest times and are being woven still as both Josephs call us to Christ.

A stunning point to ponder with Joseph and Joseph is the exceeding greatness of the second in comparison with the first. For who did most to serve an increase of life? Was it he who was appointed to run the household of the mighty magnate Potiphar, then run a royal prison, then Pharaoh's household, and indeed Egypt, the mightiest country in the world, and finally had all the world in the palm of his hand as they came begging him for bread, which is the staff of life? Or was it he who silently watched over Jesus and Mary, the devoted carpenter? Without a trace of doubt, though there be few men so awesome as the first, the second achieved immeasurably more for the life of the world. Having familial care of the infant Jesus and His Mother Mary gives an infinitely greater reach than having care of any ancient empire. St Joseph nurtured the Bread of Heaven which has been feeding the world for two thousand years and counting, for an eternal increase of life.

This, to put it mildly, is important. To know Joseph is to know St Joseph. So much does God desire that we come to know Mary and Joseph that He began telling us about them from the beginning, with poetic and evolving repetition, the focus sharpening, new details being supplemented. Through the saints God wishes to lead us to His Son, to our salvation, Jesus, יֵשׁוּעַ . He has given us His Word.

> O Blessed Joseph, happy man, to whom it was given not only to see and to hear that God Whom many kings longed to see, and saw not, to hear, and heard not; but also to carry Him in your arms, to embrace Him, to clothe Him, and guard and defend Him. Pray for us, O Blessed Joseph. That we may be made worthy of the promises of Christ.[135]

---

[135] *Oratio ad Sanctum Ioseph Ante Missam,* from the Roman Missal, recommended for daily use.

V: MEMORARE, O PIISSIMA VIRGO MARIA

T he purpose of this book is: to support invincible hope in the absolute victory of good over evil; to attest that God appointed the Virgin Mary to achieve this historically; and to make clear that all souls in all generations are called to cooperate in this greatest of works (Jn 14:12). The profound conviction that all this is true becomes supercharged when we find it written in the OT again and again and again.

God plainly promised that the serpent's head would be crushed (Gen 3:15). The textual difficulty of whether this will be accomplished by *"the woman"* or by *"her seed"*, by *"she"* or *"he"*, is resolved by accepting it is both, for Jesus lives in Mary and Mary lives in Jesus (cf. Lk 1:31; Jn 14:20; 17:21; Gal 2:20; Acts 17:28). Now from Heaven, as on Calvary, they act together. Whether we recognise the same promise of the Antichrist's demise repeated in the accounts of God acting through Jael, Judith, Esther and other OT women, depends not upon the text alone but also upon the heart of the reader. Our heart must be unveiled, spiritually circumcised, to read the Old in the light of the New, that is in the light of Christ.

Jesus defeated evil by His Death on Calvary. All His enemies failed. Jesus' Resurrection is the demonstration thereof. But what is it to God to defeat evil? It is far greater that He makes us capable of the same.

The Mother of God stood by Jesus' Cross for good reason. There within her Immaculate Heart, Our Lady also dealt an absolute defeat to evil. Mary was the only creature who had faith, hope and charity during the Crucifixion and before the Resurrection. United with Her Son in this supreme act of love, she offered Him to the Father. Wherever God's victory over evil is working through the Cross, through sacrifice, Our Lady is present and active too. This will be true at the end of time in the historical triumph of the Cross (*"In hoc signo vinces"*), which is also the triumph of Mary's Immaculate Heart. And the victory of both is won with our cooperation also in the souls of the saved, the children of God, they who like Jesus love God the Father and Mary their heavenly Mother more than their own life (see Apoc 12*ff*).

In a way, Mary's own life contains prefiguration and fulfilment, and in turn her life is a fulfilment and prefigurement. That is to say, the Immaculate Conception is a prefiguration of her defeating evil on Calvary. Calvary is a fulfilment of Mary's Immaculate Conception. And on the whole historical scale, Mary's life is a fulfilment of the Protoevangelium spoken by God to our first parents in Eden. And Mary's life is a prefiguration of the fulfilment of the Triumph of her Immaculate Heart at the end of history. If that sounds complicated, in any case, anyone who gives themself as a slave of love to Jesus through Mary can experience her victory in their own soul. This is why Our Lady revealed at Fatima on 13th July 1917 that Jesus "wants to establish in the world devotion to my Immaculate Heart". There is no better plan for salvation. Indeed, no other plan is needed.

Though the total victory of good over evil is guaranteed, it is not given to us on a plate. The various foretellings of Our Lady crushing satan's head show that we are all called to cooperate. Ten thousand saints fought for Barak while Jael achieved her crowning work. All the inhabitants of Thebez joined the woman in the tower for the victorious last stand. The friends of Jephthah's daughter mourned on the mountains with her, accompanying, not arguing against, her oblation. Representatives of all Israel carried out the plan of the wise woman in Abel, thereby uniting themselves to their estranged brothers, all the king's army sent from Judah. Judith required all her townspeople to keep from sin, to pray for her and endure. Then after her success she instructed them how to set the entire enemy army to flight. Queen Esther had all the Jews of Susa fast with her for three days and three nights before securing the saving decree from her King. Then the King asked of her what to do with her enemies and Esther directed the course of deliverance, calling up every Jew in the world who was able to fully participate. Susanna suffered anguish alone, all alone for a night, but when the final trial came the people's hearts turned back to her and they dragged her accusers to their death. All this is to demonstrate that, while our salvation comes from God through Mary, we are not mere spectators but are to fully engage.

What shall we do? The same OT which guided Mary is written for our instruction as well (Rom 15:4; 1 Cor 10:11). In combination the prefigurations clarify that this battle is not against flesh and blood but is spiritual. And precisely because it is spiritual, the ultimate victory of good over evil involves every soul ever created, including all of us today, not just the final generation.

To the first point, some complain that the OT is too bloody, too violent, too strange for their taste. Is the Virgin Mary to be likened to a hammer-wielding combatant (Jael)? Is Our Lady to be compared to a rock-hurling warrior (from Thebez)? Is the Mother of God akin to one who gives the green light for assassination (in Abel)? Is Our Lady of Sorrows related to one who decapitates a comatose man with his sword (Judith)? The answer is both 'Of course!' and 'Of course not!'

'Of course!' once we understand the fight is spiritual. But in saying it is spiritual, many may be in danger of thinking the fight is not real. The world wants safe spaces and elements within the Catholic hierarchy are aping the world: *"From the prophet even to the priest, all of them act with deceit... saying: 'Peace, peace.' And there was no peace"* (Jer 6:13-14). After decades of watered-down presentations of the Faith, now approaching apostasy in Germany's *Synodale Weg*, the OT reminds us of the violence of hammers, of millstones, of swords. Not that Heaven wants us to pick up these weapons and draw blood — 'Of course not!' — but to realise the spiritual struggle is ruthless. We have to absolutely crush sin within us, go to war against it, eradicate it. If we imagine we can win peace through dialogue with Sisera or Sheba, with Holofernes or Haman, with Abimelech or the Antichrist, we have not been paying attention. Similarly doomed is any accommodation with heresy or sin. Today, the *Synodale Weg* is set to metastasise into worldwide apostasy with Bergoglio's Synod on Synodality — if we allow it.

With everything at stake, how is it Catholics circulate saccharine pictures of Our Lady portrayed as a fairytale princess? As an advance remedy against this sentimentalism, the OT places reality before our eyes in a manner unforgettably graphic: smashed skulls; exploding brains; a severed head thrown over the wall; a neck hacked right through; ten sons hung on a fifty-foot gibbet.

Prefigurations teach by similarities and through differences. From the similarities between figure and fulfilment, we see how violent and absolute this warfare is. From the necessary differences we insist our warfare is waged not against men but against demons, against sin, against untruth. Our weapons are prayer and repentance, mortification and acts of mercy, the Sacraments and the Word of God. In apparitions Our Lady insists upon penance. This was the remedy God awarded to Adam and Eve. The same Jonah preached to the Ninivites. The same St John the Baptist preached to prepare for the Kingdom of God. The same Our Lady enjoined at Lourdes and more recently at Fatima. Doubtless the final battlefield is the whole earth as it enters the Apocalypse, but before then the war takes place in every man's soul.

By God's grace, by Mary's assistance, even in our soul the serpent will be crushed. Moses seized the snare of satan, the golden calf, pulverising it to powder (Ex 32:20). King Josiah's restoration had the demonic altars and idols torn down and smashed, ground even unto dust (2 Chron 34:4,7). This is a picture of the process which must take place in our souls, namely the pulverisation of sin. The word contrition, meaning sorrow for our sins, derives from *conterere*, to break to pieces, to grind down to dust. Consideration of Our Lady should move us to this contrition. There are some hard hearts unmoved by Jesus. They might claim He could have escaped but chose not to. They might assert that being God He could not feel pain. These thoughts are superficial and wrong-headed. But who on earth can consider Mary and remain cold? Her Son died for our sins. How we have wounded her heart! What had she ever done to deserve this treatment from us? Nothing.

In case anyone is unmoved by Mary's pain, let them read of Jephthah's daughter and see if their heart can remain untroubled. Amid vivid stories of ferocity and murder, Jephthah's daughter brings calm to show the fight is inward, spiritual. It is true she died a bloody, fiery death. However, she crushed nobody's head. At least not externally. Within her pure soul, though, the vestiges of sin were destroyed. Silently satan was crushed. Like Mary, she lifted not a finger against any human being.

That the final victory depends first upon sanctity rather than cracking someone's head open we see also in Ruth, from whom there was no violence. Her perfected nature is revealed in how she treated Naomi, and how she delighted Boaz, and how she won the admiration of the whole of Bethlehem. Ruth shows us Mary's assiduous care for the least and most hidden of God's children if we accept that grains of wheat represent souls. All we read of Ruth is positive. The way to overcome evil is by seeking the truth and loving the good.

Without Rahab the Hebrews would have found no way past Jericho. Yet there is less chance to enter Heaven without Mary than to have taken the Promised Land without Rahab's help. How is it then that some dismiss Mary? Have they not read the Prophets and Writings; are they not mindful of Rahab?

These women are offered for our meditation. They lead us to Mary who always leads us to Christ. Vitally the Virgin Mary confirmed in 1917: "In the end my Immaculate Heart will triumph." In the light of this message, we can re-read the Scriptures and find the same truth was laid down long ago.

It would be a misreading to recoil at the deceptions of Tamar or Jael, at the trickery of Judith or the plotting of Esther. Their apparent duplicity by no means recommends any dishonesty. God cannot deceive or be deceived. Rather, His Plans are so excellent they exceed the comprehension of His creatures. His willingness to use the humble is so unexpected that the arrogant have a fatal blind spot to it. Who could have guessed the Incarnation before God revealed it? Who of us could have guessed God's Son would die on the Cross to defeat death? It could never have occurred to satan that God would take our sins upon Himself, nor that the quiet woman on Calvary, tears on her cheeks, was even rejoicing in her tortured heart that God's Will was being accomplished. God deceived nobody, but evil deceived itself. So satan lost to Mary. His followers always make the same mistake and so will the Antichrist in the end.

The final, apocalyptic conflict involves every soul ever created. The struggle through history is one struggle. Whether one was born long before Christ, or whether one enjoyed the High Middle Ages, or endures today, or will be born for the time of final apostasy, all who win, win together. All who lose, hate each other. By God's grace, every act of love — ever! — contributes to the strength of the Church, forms her character to overcome evil in the last days. Every sin committed — ever! — serves the aggrandisement of evil and its antichrist claims until the measure of sin be full for its inevitable self-destruction. The victory at the end will truly belong to people from all time in whose souls love overcomes sin. And the implosion of evil will justify the eternal perdition of each of the damned, from every century, for it will be manifest to all that serving sin has conjured up hell on earth. That is, until earth pass away and the servants of evil, the last of that line of losers, have nowhere left but only the hell which is eternal.

Each of us is in this to crush the serpent's head:

> *But I want you to be wise in what is good, and simple in what is evil. And may the God of peace quickly crush Satan under your feet. The grace of our Lord Jesus Christ be with you.* (Rom 16:19-20)

As Mary triumphs at the end of history, so she triumphs in the soul of each person who comes to Heaven. God gives her for our spiritual mother. We are her offspring. We are dependent upon her. Evil will wax so strong toward the end that those who have not already established steadfast hope in God's promises will find it too disorientating to convert:

> *And there will be, on earth, distress among the Gentiles, out of confusion at the roaring of the sea and of the waves: men withering away out of fear and out of apprehension over the things that will overwhelm the whole world. For the powers of the heavens will be moved.* (Lk 21:25-26)

A rational man ought to be terrified by these things unless, turning to Christ and Our Lady, he thereby loses his fear. In the last days it will be too late, too confusing, too fearful, to begin studying the OT. But we can work on it now, not only for ourselves, that we may stand whenever our own end comes, but also out of charity for those after us, ripening now the Marian culture for future generations to inherit.

Besides, each one of us faces an end, and we will want Mary by us in our final hour, be that the hour of our death or the hour of the end of the world.

The conclusion is contained in the principles. When Adam and Eve thought themselves utterly lost, forlorn following their fall, God did not wait even one whole day before announcing a Saviour who would contend with their adversary, and a woman who would seal the Saviour's victory. He spoke His sentence on the serpent in their presence, that the woman *"will crush your head"*. The whole world is meant to hear these words.

In order that mankind does not forget, that we never lose hope, the theme of a woman crushing the head of the wicked is presented again and again in the OT and developed in unforgettable detail. Even when faced with existential threats to their whole people, even when evil seemed unstoppable, even when salvation seemed unattainable, these women, by God's grace, won through.

All this is spoken to us now, and vitally for the last generation who will suffer the worst persecutions, so that despite seemingly insurmountable evil, we do not waver in faith, for the many prefigurations serve as so many promises from God. We may recall that by God's promises Abraham *"believed, with a hope beyond hope"* (Rom 4:18). So also did Mary. We need their faith!

Help is at hand, inspiration from those souls who acted alone (Jael) and in a melee (in Thebez), were young (Jephthah's virgin daughter) and old (woman of Abel), Gentile (Ruth) and Jew (Maccabean Mother), prostitute (Rahab) and chaste wife (Susanna), Empress (Esther) and mother (Tamar), widow (Judith) and devoted Queen (Bathsheba). Somehow Mary gathers up all their lives for the perfect finish, as she gathers all loving souls to present them to her Sovereign Son in Heaven.

Are we willing to bow to Mary as Queen of Heaven? It was this that satan and the fallen angels were not willing to do. They thought: "I would rather be damned than bow to that woman." Do we not face the same test? For there are not two hierarchies in Heaven, one of angels and one of men. Rather there is one combined hierarchy, saints and angels together, all cleaving to God.[136] All creatures in Heaven have the same Head, Jesus Christ, and the same Queen, His Mother. Are we willing to accept Mary as Queen of Heaven, and so to honour her, obey her, rejoice in her?

God is pleased when we trust in His ways. This is more precious when we are most pressed. For a firmer foundation, we can glean saving truths from the Bible that are not apparent from the world around us when times are desperate. In the last days it will appear as if all hope is lost. By reading the Bible now while it is still day, and meditating on the prefigurations God buried there, we become convinced of its truth, taste this in our soul, experience it in our life, so hope becomes

---

[136] St Augustine, *De Civitate Dei XII*, 9. Also St Thomas, *II Sent.*, d.IX q.1 a.8 ad 4.

invincible. Then when everything external falls apart, we may be found standing under the Cross with Mary, our hearts completely one with hers and the Most Sacred Heart of Jesus. Their victory is ours to share.

> Remember, O most gracious Virgin Mary, that never was it known that anyone who fled to thy protection, implored thy help, or sought thy intercession was left unaided. Inspired with this confidence, I fly to thee, O Virgin of virgins, my Mother; to thee do I come; before thee I stand, sinful and sorrowful. O Mother of the Word Incarnate, despise not my petitions, but in thy mercy hear and answer me. Amen.[137]

---

[137] *Memorare, O piissima Virgo Maria.*

About the Author

Born in 1973, James Mawdsley grew up in Lancashire, England. He is author of *The Heart Must Break: The Fight for Democracy and Truth in Burma* (Century, 2001), detailing his three detentions as a political prisoner in Burma. During seventeen months of solitary confinement he received the Bible which helped turn his cell from "hell to heaven" and without which this current book would doubtless not have been written.

From 2003 to 2004, having met former prisoners and guards who had defected from North Korea, Mawdsley served as the first Secretariat to the British-North Korean All-Party Parliamentary Group, sitting in on high-level political-military meetings in Pyongyang and London. His priority in arranging these exchanges was to challenge the North Korean government regarding their gulag system.

Slowly realising the futility of political attempts to overcome evil unless Jesus Christ is honoured as King of Kings, Mawdsley was surprised on 3rd September 2005 by a crystal-clear call to the priesthood. He was ordained a Catholic priest in 2016 for the traditional Roman rite.

Fr Mawdsley is forever grateful to his formators for guiding him deeper into the inexhaustible graces found in Scripture and Tradition.